Unreal Engine 4 Game Development Essentials

Master the basics of Unreal Engine 4 to build stunning video games

Satheesh PV

BIRMINGHAM - MUMBAI

Unreal Engine 4 Game Development Essentials

First published: February 2016

Production reference: 1220216

Published by Packt Publishing Ltd.
Livery Place
35 Livery Street
Birmingham B3 2PB, UK.

ISBN 978-1-78439-196-6

www.packtpub.com

Cover image by Satheesh PV (mindfreak2040@gmail.com)

Credits

Author
Satheesh PV

Reviewer
Omer Shapira

Commissioning Editor
Edward Bowkett

Acquisition Editor
Kevin Colaco

Content Development Editor
Deepti Thore

Technical Editor
Deepti Tuscano

Copy Editor
Merilyn Pereira

Project Coordinator
Dinesh Rathe

Proofreader
Safis Editing

Indexer
Rekha Nair

Graphics
Jason Monterio

Production Coordinator
Aparna Bhagat

Cover Work
Aparna Bhagat

About the Author

Satheesh PV is a game programmer living in Mumbai, India. He was selected by Epic Games as one of the closed beta testers for Unreal Engine 4 before its public release. He started his career as a game developer in 2012 by making a first person multiplayer game with his brother and close friend using Unreal Development Kit. He also created Unreal X-Editor, which was an IDE developed for UnrealScript, the native scripting language of Unreal Engine 3. He is also a moderator at Unreal Engine forums as well as a spotlight member and engine contributor.

Acknowledgements

I am using this opportunity to thank God for giving me talent and a wonderful family, who are my real inspiration. I am grateful to them for their aspiring guidance and continuous support while writing this book. I am thankful to Epic Games for giving out such an amazing Engine to the world for free! You guys are the best!

I express my warm thanks to my fiancée Gale Fernandes; without her amazing support and constructive criticism, this book possibly would not have happened.

I would also like to thank my brother Rakesh PV for introducing me to the world of games and game technologies. It is through him I learned everything related to games and I am proud to say that he is my first mentor.

I wish to extend my deep thanks and gratitude to my good friends Alexander Paschall (Epic Games) and Chance Ivey (Epic Games) and also to my best friend Reni Dev, with whom I created my first game.

I also wish to thank my dear friend and C++ mentor, Nathan Iyer (Rama) for his great support. With his amazing articles and examples on C++, he has taught many (including me) in the Unreal Community. He was kind enough to review my C++ chapter, point out mistakes and gave honest feedbacks including spending his valuable time to remove some technical discrepancies. Thank you so much Rama! You can visit his website at: http://ue4code.com/

Finally, I would like to thank Vasundhara Devi and Lucy Fernandes for giving me all those joyous moments that put a smile on my face. Thank you moms! I love you.

About the Reviewer

Omer Shapira is an artist, software developer, and virtual reality researcher. He has worked on Game Engine projects for Nike, Google, Microsoft, Disney, Universal Pictures, and Samsung. His projects and collaborations have been exhibited at Sundance Festival, The Atlantic, The New York Times, The Guardian, Wired, Adage, and Eyebeam, and have won awards from Tribeca Film Festival, Ars Electronica, the Art Directors Club, and The Webbys.

Omer is currently head of virtual reality and game engines at Fake Love, an experiential design studio. Previously, he worked as a developer at Framestore, The NYU Media Research Lab, and the MIT Media Lab, and as a filmmaker and VFX artist for Channel 10. Omer studied mathematics at Tel Aviv University and human-computer interaction at New York University.

Omer's four-dimensional video game, Horizon (written in Unreal Engine), will be released in 2017.

You can find him at omershapira.com.

I'd like to thank the people who contributed the most to my ability to write game engines: Ken Perlin, Casey Muratori, Jonathan Blow, Fred Ford, and Paul Reiche III.

I'd like to thank Surya Mattu and Jenn Schiffer for being good parents, and my cat, Nitzu.

www.PacktPub.com

eBooks, discount offers, and more

Did you know that Packt offers eBook versions of every book published, with PDF and ePub files available? You can upgrade to the eBook version at www.PacktPub.com and as a print book customer, you are entitled to a discount on the eBook copy. Get in touch with us at customercare@packtpub.com for more details.

At www.PacktPub.com, you can also read a collection of free technical articles, sign up for a range of free newsletters and receive exclusive discounts and offers on Packt books and eBooks.

https://www2.packtpub.com/books/subscription/packtlib

Do you need instant solutions to your IT questions? PacktLib is Packt's online digital book library. Here, you can search, access, and read Packt's entire library of books.

Why subscribe?

- Fully searchable across every book published by Packt
- Copy and paste, print, and bookmark content
- On demand and accessible via a web browser

Table of Contents

Preface

The purpose of *Unreal Engine 4 Game Development Essentials* is to teach people interested in using Unreal Engine how to create video games. You will learn what Unreal Engine is and how to download and use it. From there, we will go through the collection of tools available in Unreal Engine 4 including Materials, Blueprints, Matinee, UMG, C++, and more.

What this book covers

Chapter 1, *Introduction to Unreal Engine 4*, is where we begin our journey on *Unreal Engine 4 Game Development Essentials*. In this chapter, the reader will learn how and where to download Unreal Engine as well as the difference between the source version and launcher version. After the Engine's installation (or compilation, if it was the source version) we will get comfortable with the user interface of Unreal Engine. We will also learn about the basics of Content Browser, BSP, and how to change the splash screen and the icons for your game.

Chapter 2, *Importing Assets*, teaches how to import your custom FBX assets into Unreal Engine once we get the Engine up and running. You will learn about collisions, materials, and the level of detail.

Chapter 3, *Materials*, teaches you about the Material editor and some common nodes used to create shaders for your assets. After learning the basics of Material, we will create an example material function that can change the intensity of a normal map.

Chapter 4, *Post Process*, continues to post-processing after teaching you about materials. In this chapter, you will learn how to override the default post process settings. After that, we will learn how to add our own post process volume and learn a simple but very powerful feature called LUT. After that, we will create a special material that can be used with post process, and this material will have the ability to highlight user-defined objects in the world.

Chapter 5, Lights, gets us halfway through our *Unreal Engine 4 Game Development Essentials* journey, and this chapter will introduce you to the lighting system. We start of by covering the basics, such as placing lights and going through the common settings. You will then learn more about the Lightmass Global Illumination system, including how to properly prepare a UV channel for your asset to be used with Lightmass. By the end of this chapter, you will learn how to build your scene with Lightmass as well as Lightmass settings.

Chapter 6, Blueprints, teaches you what Blueprints are and about the various types of Blueprints that are available in the Engine. Blueprints are Unreal Engine's number one tool that allows artists and designers to quickly prototype their game (or even make one!). You will also learn about the different graph types, such as event graph, function graph, macro graph, and so on, and how to spawn a Blueprint dynamically at runtime.

Chapter 7, Matinee, looks at the cinematic side of Unreal Engine 4 and the tool associated with it, called Matinee. You will learn what Matinee is, how to create one, and get familiar with the UI. After the basics, we will learn how to manipulate objects in Matinee as well as create a very basic cutscene, which we will trigger using Blueprints.

Chapter 8, Unreal Motion Graphics, teaches you to create a basic HUD that shows the health of the player. Unreal Motion Graphics (UMG) is the UI authoring tool in Unreal Engine. UMG is used to create Player HUD, Main Menu, Pause Menu, and so on. You will also learn how to create 3D widgets, which can be placed in the world or attached to an actor class.

Chapter 9, Particles, looks at the extremely powerful and robust tool called cascade particle editor and creates a particle system, as no game is good without good visual effects. We then combine this with simple Blueprint scripting to create randomly bursting particles.

Chapter 10, Introduction to Unreal C++, goes over C++ as we draw close to the end of our *Unreal Engine 4 Game Development Essentials* journey. In this chapter, you will learn how to get Visual Studio 2015 Community Edition and learn the basics of C++ by inspecting the Third Person Template character class. We will then extend this class to add support for health and the health regeneration system. You will also learn how to expose variables and functions to Blueprint Editor.

Chapter 11, Packaging Project, brings us to the end of our *Unreal Engine 4 Game Development Essentials* journey. In this final chapter, we will recap all the things we've done, including a few tips, and finally, you will learn how to create a release version of your game.

What you need for this book

Unreal Engine 4.9 or higher

Who this book is for

This book is aimed at anyone who is interested in learning game development using Unreal Engine 4. If you are passionate about developing games and want to know about the essentials of Unreal Engine 4 and its tools, then this book will get you up and running quickly. Unreal Engine 4 will be your next step towards creating next gen video games for all platforms, including mobile and consoles.

Conventions

In this book, you will find a number of text styles that distinguish between different kinds of information. Here are some examples of these styles and an explanation of their meaning.

Code words in text, database table names, folder names, filenames, file extensions, pathnames, dummy URLs, user input, and Twitter handles are shown as follows: "This adds or removes a path (it can be a virtual package path such as \Game\ MyContent\ or an absolute path such as C:\My Contents) for the engine to monitor new content."

A block of code is set as follows:

```
void APACKT_CPPCharacter::RegenerateHealth()
{
    if (Health >= GetClass()->GetDefaultObject<ABaseCharacter>()-
>Health)
    {
        Health = GetClass()->GetDefaultObject<ABaseCharacter>()-
>Health;
    }
    else
    {
        Health += RegenerateAmount;
        FTimerHandle TimerHandle_ReRunRegenerateHealth;
        GetWorldTimerManager().SetTimer( TimerHandle_
ReRunRegenerateHealth, this, &APACKT_CPPCharacter::RegenerateHealth,
RegenDelay );
    }
}
```

New terms and **important words** are shown in bold. Words that you see on the screen, for example, in menus or dialog boxes, appear in the text like this: "Once you log in, you can download the launcher by clicking on the big orange **Download** button under **Get Unreal Engine**."

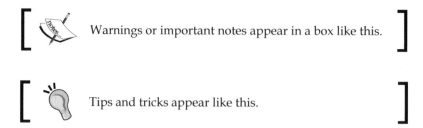

Warnings or important notes appear in a box like this.

Tips and tricks appear like this.

Reader feedback

Feedback from our readers is always welcome. Let us know what you think about this book—what you liked or disliked. Reader feedback is important for us as it helps us develop titles that you will really get the most out of.

To send us general feedback, simply e-mail feedback@packtpub.com, and mention the book's title in the subject of your message.

If there is a topic that you have expertise in and you are interested in either writing or contributing to a book, see our author guide at www.packtpub.com/authors.

Customer support

Now that you are the proud owner of a Packt book, we have a number of things to help you to get the most from your purchase.

Downloading the example code

You can download the example code files for this book from your account at http://www.packtpub.com. If you purchased this book elsewhere, you can visit http://www.packtpub.com/support and register to have the files e-mailed directly to you.

You can download the code files by following these steps:

1. Log in or register to our website using your e-mail address and password.
2. Hover the mouse pointer on the **SUPPORT** tab at the top.
3. Click on **Code Downloads & Errata**.
4. Enter the name of the book in the **Search** box.
5. Select the book for which you're looking to download the code files.
6. Choose from the drop-down menu where you purchased this book from.
7. Click on **Code Download**.

Once the file is downloaded, please make sure that you unzip or extract the folder using the latest version of:

- WinRAR / 7-Zip for Windows
- Zipeg / iZip / UnRarX for Mac
- 7-Zip / PeaZip for Linux

Downloading the color images of this book

We also provide you with a PDF file that has color images of the screenshots/diagrams used in this book. The color images will help you better understand the changes in the output. You can download this file from `http://www.packtpub.com/sites/default/files/downloads/UnrealEngine4GameDevelopment Essentials_ColorImages.pdf`.

Errata

Although we have taken every care to ensure the accuracy of our content, mistakes do happen. If you find a mistake in one of our books—maybe a mistake in the text or the code—we would be grateful if you could report this to us. By doing so, you can save other readers from frustration and help us improve subsequent versions of this book. If you find any errata, please report them by visiting `http://www.packtpub.com/submit-errata`, selecting your book, clicking on the **Errata Submission Form** link, and entering the details of your errata. Once your errata are verified, your submission will be accepted and the errata will be uploaded to our website or added to any list of existing errata under the Errata section of that title.

To view the previously submitted errata, go to `https://www.packtpub.com/books/content/support` and enter the name of the book in the search field. The required information will appear under the **Errata** section.

Piracy

Piracy of copyrighted material on the Internet is an ongoing problem across all media. At Packt, we take the protection of our copyright and licenses very seriously. If you come across any illegal copies of our works in any form on the Internet, please provide us with the location address or website name immediately so that we can pursue a remedy.

Please contact us at copyright@packtpub.com with a link to the suspected pirated material.

We appreciate your help in protecting our authors and our ability to bring you valuable content.

Questions

If you have a problem with any aspect of this book, you can contact us at questions@packtpub.com, and we will do our best to address the problem.

1
Introduction to Unreal Engine 4

Welcome to *Unreal Engine 4 Game Development Essentials*. In this chapter, you will learn how to download Unreal Engine's source version and launcher version. After that, we will get familiar with the Unreal Engine 4 UI and Content Browser.

Unreal Engine 4 download

Unreal Engine 4 is completely free (including all future updates!) to download and use. You get all the Unreal Engine tools, free sample contents, complete C++ source code which includes code for the entire editor, and all of its tools; you also get access to official documentation that includes tutorials and support resources, plus you get access to UE4 marketplace, which offers tons of free and commercial content.

Unreal Engine 4 can be downloaded in two different versions. One is a binary version (launcher) and the other is the source version (GitHub). The differences between the GitHub and launcher version are as follows:

- **Launcher (binary) version**: These are compiled by Epic and are available through launcher. You will also get all source files (*.cpp) with the launcher version, but you cannot make any modifications to Unreal Engine since launcher versions do not generate a solution file.

- **GitHub version**: These do not have any binary files so you have to compile the Engine yourself. You get the entire source and you can modify virtually anything in Unreal Engine. You can add new Engine features, modify existing features or remove them (which no one does), and create a pull request on GitHub so if Epic likes it, they will integrate it officially into Unreal Engine.

In this guide, I'll show you how to get both versions.

Downloading the launcher version

To download the launcher version of Unreal Engine, you obviously need the launcher. To download the launcher, follow these steps:

1. First go to `https://www.unrealengine.com/` and log in using your credentials.

2. Once you log in, you can download the launcher by clicking on the big orange **Download** button under **Get Unreal Engine**.

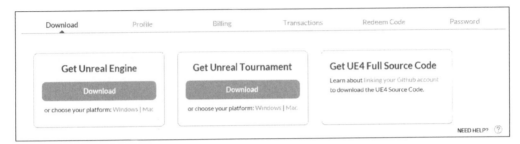

When you open the launcher for the first time after installation, it should automatically download the latest version of Unreal Engine 4. If it doesn't, then go to the **Library** tab and click on **Add Engine**. A new Engine slot will now appear and here, you can select your Unreal Engine version and install it.

Downloading the GitHub version

To download the source of Unreal Engine 4, follow these steps

1. First create a GitHub account (it's free!).
2. After that, you need to go to `https://www.unrealengine.com/dashboard/settings` and update your GitHub account name and click on **Save**:

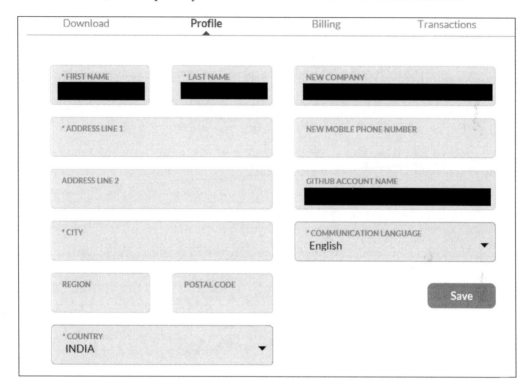

Forking Unreal Engine repository

After you have successfully linked your GitHub account with your Unreal Engine account, you need to log in to GitHub and navigate to the Unreal Engine repository.

Make sure you have linked your GitHub account to your Unreal Engine account. Otherwise, you will not be able to see the Unreal Engine repository.

When you are at the repository page:

1. Click on **Fork** at the top right of the page.

2. Select your username to fork it to your GitHub repository.

3. Then, you need to download GitHub for Windows (if you are on Windows) or GitHub for Mac (if you are on Mac) and install it.

You need this Git client to clone (download) your forked repository, make your own changes to Unreal Engine, and submit the changes as a pull request to Epic to integrate them into the editor.

To clone your forked repository follow these steps:

1. Start GitHub and log in using your credentials.

2. Click on the plus (+) sign on the top left corner of the Git client.

3. Then, click on the **Clone** tab and select your **username** (you should now see Unreal Engine).

4. Now, click on **Clone** Unreal Engine and choose a folder where you want to save your Unreal Engine repository.

5. Click on **OK**.

6. You should now see GitHub cloning Unreal Engine to your hard disk.

Once cloning is complete, navigate to that directory and run the `Setup.bat` file.

1. This will download all the necessary files that are needed to compile the engine and will also install all the required prerequisites for the Engine.

2. This might take some time depending on your Internet speed because it has to download more than 2 GB of files.

Compiling Unreal Engine

Once `Setup.bat` has finished, run `GenerateProjectFiles.bat`, which will generate the Visual Studio Solution file. Open the `UE4.sln` file and now, you are all set to compile your own copy of Unreal Engine 4☺. Now, right-click on UE4 in the **Solution Explorer** and click on **Build**.

This will take from 15 minutes to 1 hour depending on your system hardware. So sit back, grab a cup of coffee, and wait till Engine finishes compiling.

Getting familiar with Unreal Engine

Once your Engine finishes compiling (or downloading, if you are using launcher) it's time to start it:

- **Starting your custom build**: You can either press *F5* in Visual Studio to start debugging the Engine or navigate to the directory where you downloaded it and go to `Engine\Binaries\Win64` folder and double-click on `UE4Editor.exe`.

- **Starting launcher build**: Simply click on that big **Launch** button and you're good to go.

You might experience long loading time when you start the Engine for the first time after compiling. This is because Unreal Engine will optimize the contents for your platform to derive data cache. This is a one-time process.

After the splash screen, you should now see the Unreal project browser. Perform the following steps:

1. Select the **New Project** tab, and this is where you create your new projects.

2. For this book, we will stick with a **Blank Blueprint Project**. So, in the **Blueprint** tab, select **Blank** project.

3. You can choose which platform you want for your project. There are two platforms available: **Desktop/Console** and **Mobile/Tablet**. Feel free to change this setting for your project. The second setting determines the graphics settings for your platform. If you choose **Desktop/Console**, it's better to stick with **Maximum Quality** and if your project is targeting **Mobile/Tablets**, you should choose scalable 3D or 2D, which is aimed at low-end GPUs. The third and final setting lets you add some **Starter Content** from Epic, which contains some basic meshes, materials, and textures. You can choose not to include **Starter Content** so the project will only contain essential elements for the selected project.

4. Note that it is not recommended to include **Starter Content** when creating a project for the **Mobile/Tablet** platform. This can significantly increase the package size of your project.

5. Choose a name for your project and the location where you want to save it.

6. Finally, click on **Create Project** to start Unreal Engine 4 with your project:

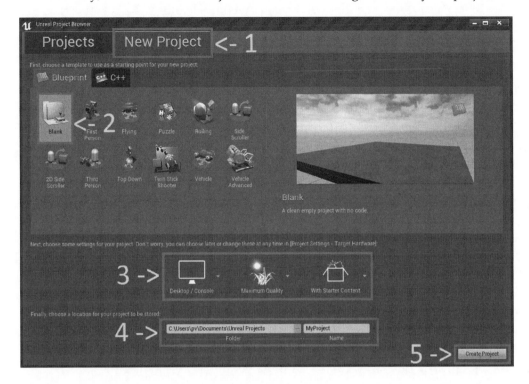

This is how the Unreal Engine user interface looks:

Once Unreal Engine starts up, you should see a scene similar to the preceding screenshot. This is the scene that will be displayed by default, if you choose to include **Starter Content**. If you skip **Starter Content**, then the startup scene will be different.

The viewport toolbar

The viewport toolbar contains various tools that you will use throughout your level design process. Let's take a quick look at them:

- **Transform Tools**: These three tools are the move tool, the rotate tool, and the scale tool.

- **Coordinate System**: This allows you to move, rotate, or scale your Actor either on world axes (world space) or on its own local axes (local space). By default, Unreal editor starts in world axes but you can toggle by clicking on the icon. The globe icon means world space and the cube icon means local space.

- **Snapping and Move Grid**: Snapping allows you to snap one Actor to another Actor's surface, and move grid allows you to snap to a three-dimensional implicit grid within the scene.

- **Rotation Grid**: This provides incremental rotation snaps.

- **Scale Grid**: This snaps to additive increments.

 Snapping preferences for move, rotate, and scale can be adjusted in **Editor Preferences**. Go to **Edit | Editor Preferences | Viewports** and then scroll to **Grid Snapping Category**.

- **Camera Speed**: This lets you control how fast the camera moves in viewport.

 You can fine-tune the camera speed by holding down the right mouse button (while using *WASD* controls) and scrolling the mouse wheel up or down to speed up or slow down the camera's movement.

- **Maximize Viewport**: This toggles between a single viewport and a 4-view split style.

You can adjust the layout of **Viewport** by changing the **Layout** option, as shown in the following screenshot:

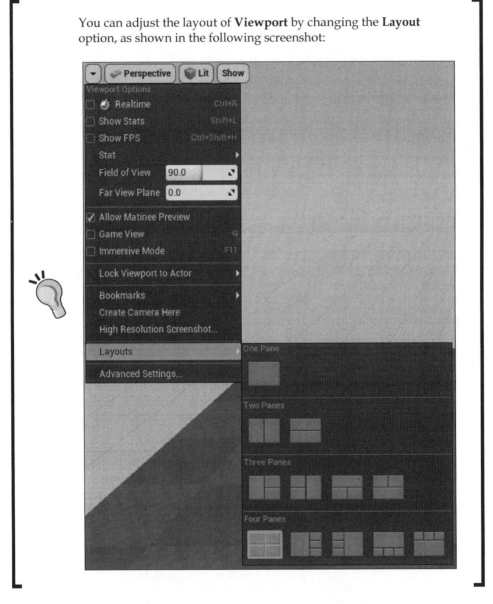

Later in this chapter, you will learn how to use **Binary Space Partitioning (BSP)** and change some project settings such as **Splash** screen, game **Icon**, and so on.

Modes

The **Modes** tab contains all five modes of the editor. They are as follows:

- **Place** mode (shortcut key is *Shift + 1*): **Place** mode allows you to quickly place your recently placed objects and also Engine primitives such as lights, geometries, triggers, volumes, and so on.

- **Paint** mode (shortcut key is *Shift + 2*): **Paint** mode (also known as **Mesh Paint**) allows you to interactively paint vertex colors on **Static Mesh** in **Level Viewport**.

- **Landscape** mode (shortcut key is *Shift + 3*): **Landscape** mode lets you create a new landscape entirely in Unreal Editor or import a height map from an external program, such as **World Machine**, **TerreSculptor**, and so on, and make modifications to it.

- **Foliage** mode (shortcut key is *Shift + 4*): **Foliage** mode allows you to paint or erase multiple static meshes on **Landscapes**, other static meshes, and so on. An example workflow is to paint grass, trees, and so on on a large area.

- **Geometry Editing** mode (shortcut key is *Shift + 5*): **Geometry** mode allows you to edit BSP brushes.

Content Browser

Content Browser is what you call the heart of your project. This is where you create, import, view, edit, organize, and modify all the assets for your game. It also lets you rename, delete, copy, and move assets across other folders just like you do in Windows Explorer. Additionally, Content Browser also lets you search for specific assets based on keywords or asset type and you can exclude assets from your search by adding '-' (hyphen) as the prefix.

You can also create **Collections** to arrange your commonly used assets for quick access.

 Collections are just references to assets and are not moved into collections. That means a single asset can exist in multiple collections and you can create an unlimited number of collections.

There are three types of collections:

* **Shared collection**: These are visible to you and to other users. This option is active only if you have **Source Control** (for example: Perforce, Subversion and so on.) enabled.

* **Private collection**: These are visible only to those who are invited to view the collection. This option is active only if you have **Source Control** (for example: Perforce, Subversion and so on.) enabled.

* **Local collection**: These are only for you. That means they only exist on your local machine.

If you want to transfer an asset from one project to another, you can right-click on the asset and choose **Migrate...**, which will copy that asset and all its dependencies to your new project.

Content Browser can be accessed by pressing *Ctrl+Shift+F* or from the **Windows** menu on the menu bar. You can also have four instances of **Content Browser** at the same time.

This can be really useful when you want to move assets to different folders or to preview various assets in different folders.

Content Browser view options

View options lets you do the following:

- Change the thumbnail size
- Change the view style
- Modify the 3D thumbnail, and more

View Options can be accessed from the bottom-right corner of **Content Browser**.

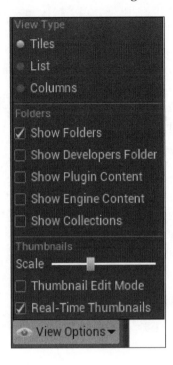

World outliner

World Outliner shows all the Actors within the level in a tree view. Actors can be selected and modified from world outliner. Right-clicking on an Actor in **World Outliner** will show the same context menu used in **Viewport** so you can modify it without having to navigate to them in **Viewport**. You can drag an Actor to another Actor and attach them together.

World outliner allows you to search for a specific Actor. You can exclude a specific Actor by adding - (hyphen) before the search term and you can force a term to match exactly by adding + before the search term.

Details panel

The **Details** panel shows all the information, utilities, and functions specific to the selection in the viewport. It displays all the editable properties for the selected Actor and provides additional functionality based on the selected Actor. For example, if you select a **Blueprint**, the **Details** panel will show everything related to that Blueprint, that is exposed variables, Blutility events, and so on. If you select a **Static Mesh** actor, the **Details** panel will show which material was applied, the collision settings, the physics settings, the rendering settings, and more. The **Details** panel can be locked to the selected Actor so it does not change based on Actor selection. Just like **Content Browser**, you can have four instances of **Details** panel open at the same time.

Navigating the Viewport

You can navigate the viewport easily using the mouse and keyboard.
A high-level explanation of navigating the viewport can be found here:
`https://docs.unrealengine.com/latest/INT/Engine/UI/LevelEditor/`
`Viewports/ViewportControls/index.html`

At the bottom-left corner of the viewport, there is a small question mark button. If you click on that, you will see some commonly used viewport shortcut keys.

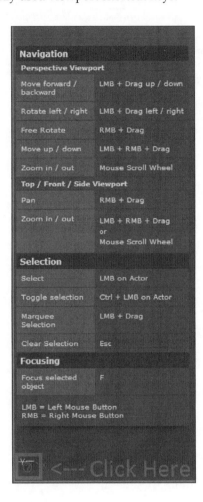

BSP

Now that we have some solid understanding of Engine UI, let's use BSP to create a simple level. BSP is a geometry tool (also known as **Geometry Brush** or simply **Brush**) used for quickly prototyping levels (also known as blocking out levels). Some developers prefer to call this **Constructive Solid Geometry (CSG)**, which is the more accurate term since geometry in Unreal editor is created by adding and subtracting brushes. BSP has been there since the first release of Unreal. It was used for level designing long ago but later, this role has been passed to static meshes because BSP is more expensive in performance.

So basically, BSP should only be used to prototype a level. Once you have the basic idea of how a level should look, you should start replacing it with static meshes.

[CSG and BSP are used interchangeably to refer the geometry in Unreal. Both are the same.]

Creating BSP

Unreal Engine 4 comes with seven Brushes and all of them can be customized in **Details** panel. They are as follows:

- **Box**: You can adjust the *X*, *Y*, and *Z* axes and set it to **Hollow**, which is a fast way to make a room, and adjust **Wall Thickness**, which defines the thickness of the inside walls.

- **Cone**: You can customize the number of sides, height, and both outer and inner radius in **Details** panel. You can also set this to **Hollow** and adjust **Wall Thickness** to define the thickness of the inside walls.

- **Cylinder**: You can customize the number of sides, height, and both outer and inner radius in **Details** panel. You can also set this to **Hollow** and adjust **Wall Thickness** to define the thickness of the inside walls.

- **Curved Stair**: This creates a staircase shape that bends around an angle but cannot wrap over itself.

- **Linear Stair**: This creates a straight staircase that does not bend.

- **Spiral Stair**: This creates a spiral staircase that can repeatedly wrap over itself.

- **Sphere**: This creates a sphere shape. The radius can be customized in **Details** panel.

Just like any other actor, you can use **Transform Tools** to move, rotate, and scale as you see fit.

There are two types of **Brushes**. They are as follows:

- **Additive**: These brushes are solid. This will *add* geometry to the level. For example, you will use the **Additive** type to create walls, floors, ceilings, and so on.

- **Subtractive**: These brushes are hollow. This will *subtract* solid space from a previously created **Additive** brush. For example, you will use the **Subtractive** type to create windows or doors on walls.

You can also convert BSP geometry to **Static Mesh** and save them in **Content Browser**, but remember, they will have no UVs or additional Material elements. It is also worth mentioning that this is not a good or recommended workflow. You should only use BSP to block out your level and later, you should import your assets created from a DCC application.

 You can go to **Geometry Editing** mode (*Shift+F5*) to edit vertices and create a custom shape.

Default starting level, splash screen, and game icon

You can change the default starting level for both the game and editor. For example, for the game you may want the **Main Menu** map as the default and for editor you want another level as the default startup level.

It's easy to set them in Unreal editor:

1. Click on **Edit** in the menu bar.
2. Click on **Project Settings**.
3. Go to **Maps & Modes**.

4. Here, you can change the game and editor default map.

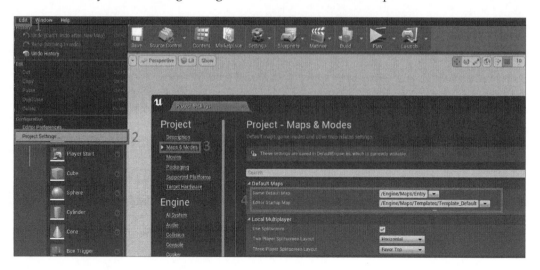

You can adjust **Splash** screen through **Project Settings**:

1. Go to **Windows** sections.

2. Change the **Splash** screen and the game **Icon** from here.

 The default dimensions for **Splash** screens are **600 x 200** and requires a **.bmp** image. The game **Icon** requires a **256 x 256** . ICO file.

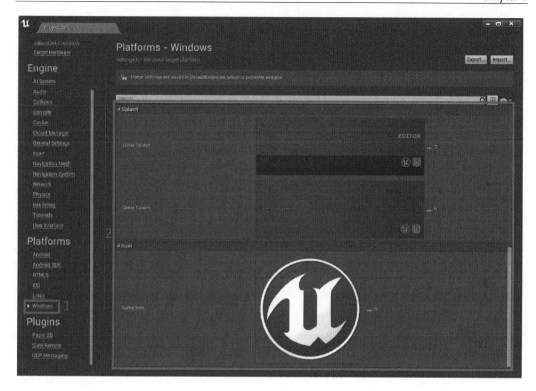

Summary

Now that you understand the basics of Unreal Engine, it's time to import some assets from a DCC application such as 3ds Max, Maya, or Blender. In the next chapter, we will create a simple mesh in 3ds Max and import it into Unreal Engine and go through various options, such as setting up materials, collisions, and LODs.

2
Importing Assets

In the previous chapter, you learned the basics of Unreal Engine. In this chapter, you will learn about importing assets from Autodesk 3ds Max.

Creating asset in a DCC application

In the previous chapter, you learned how to use BSP to block out a level. However, we need to replace them with static meshes for better performance and more control of materials, collisions, and so on. We will create models in the **Digital Content Creation** (**DCC**) application (such as Autodesk 3ds Max, Autodesk Maya, Blender, and so on) that are imported into Unreal Engine through Content Browser. Unreal Engine supports the import of both FBX and OBJ but its recommended to use the FBX format.

The following screenshot is an example asset that I will use in this chapter:

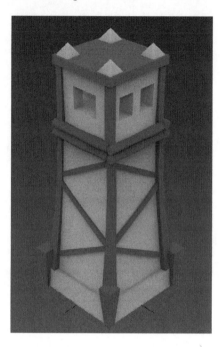

 Note that at the time of writing this book, Unreal Engine import pipeline uses FBX 2014. Trying to import using a different version might result in incompatibilities.

A few things that you need to keep in mind when modeling are as follows:

- **Units**: **Unreal Units (UU)** are critical when modeling assets for games. Incorrect units will result in assets looking larger or smaller than they are supposed to look. 1 Unreal Unit is equal to 1 cm. The sample character that comes with Unreal Engine 4 is 196 cm high. So when you are modeling assets for Unreal Engine 4, it's best to use a box that is 196 cm high as reference.

 To learn how to change units for Autodesk 3ds Max, you can refer to https://knowledge.autodesk.com/support/3ds-max/learn-explore/caas/CloudHelp/cloudhelp/2015/ENU/3DSMax/files/GUID-69E92759-6CD9-4663-B993-635D081853D2-htm.html.

To learn how to change units for Blender, you can refer to http://www.katsbits.com/tutorials/blender/metric-imperial-units.php.

- **Pivot Point**: This represents the local center and local coordinate system of an object. When you import a mesh into Unreal Engine, the pivot point of that mesh (as it was in your DCC application) determines the point where any transformation (such as move, rotate, and scale) will be performed. Generally, it is best to keep your meshes at origin (0, 0, 0) and set your pivot point to one corner of the mesh for proper alignment in Unreal Engine.

- **Triangulation**: Remember that, the Unreal Engine importer will automatically convert the quads to triangles so there is no skipping from triangles.

- **UV**: When you do UVs for assets, you can go beyond the 0-1 space, especially when you are dealing with big objects. UV channel 1 (which is channel 0 in Unreal) is used for texturing and UV channel 2 (which is channel 1 in Unreal) is used for lightmaps.

Creating collision meshes

You can create collision meshes and export them with your asset. Unreal Engine 4 provides a collision generator for static meshes but there are times when we have to create our own custom collision shapes especially if the mesh has an opening (such as doors or walls with window cutouts). In this section, we will see both options.

 Collision shapes should always stay simple because it is much faster to calculate simple shapes.

Custom collision shapes

Collision meshes are identified by Unreal importer based on their names. There are three types of collision shapes that you can define. They are as follows:

- **UBX_MeshName**: UBX stands for Unreal Box and as the name says, it should be in a box shape. You cannot move the vertices in any way or else it will not work.

- **USP_MeshName**: USP stands for Unreal Sphere and as the name says, it should be in the sphere shape. The number of segments of this sphere does not matter (although somewhere around 6-10 seems to be good) but you cannot move any vertices around.

- **UCX_MeshName**: UCX stands for Unreal Convex and as the name says, it should be a convex shape and should not be hollow or dented. This is the most commonly used collision shape because basic shapes such as boxes and spheres can be generated right inside Unreal.

In the following screenshot, you can see the red wireframe object, which is what I created for the collision shape:

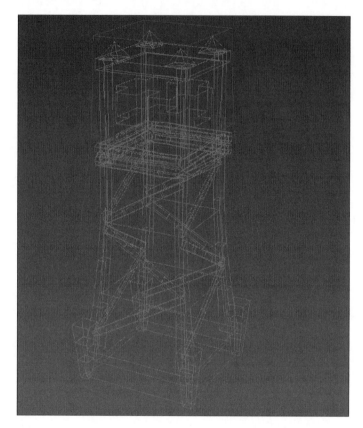

Unreal Engine 4 collision generator

Collision shapes for static meshes can be generated inside the static mesh editor. To open this editor, double-click on a static mesh asset in **Content Browser** and click on the **Collision** menu, which will then list all the options for **Collision**.

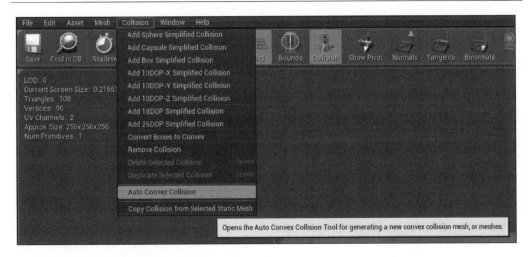

Simple shapes

The first three options in this menu are simple shapes and they are as follows:

- **Sphere Collision**: This creates a simple sphere collision shape
- **Capsule Collision**: This creates a simple capsule collision shape
- **Box Collision**: This creates a simple box collision shape

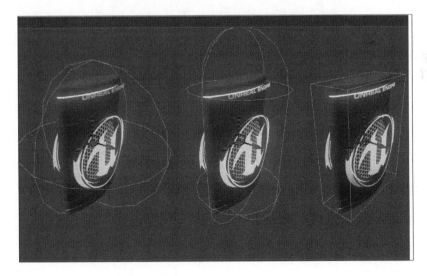

K-DOP shapes

K Discrete Oriented Polytope (K-DOP) shapes are basically bounding volumes. The numbers (10, 18, and 26) represents the K-axis aligned planes.

Auto convex collision

This option is used to create much more accurate collision shapes for your models. Once you click on this option, a new dock window appears at the bottom-right corner of static mesh editor; using **Max Hulls** (the number of hulls to be created to best match the shape of the object) and **Max Hull Verts** (which determines the complexity of the collision hulls) you can create more complex collision shapes for your **Static Mesh**.

As you can see in the following screenshot, the auto convex result is reasonably accurate:

Collision shapes support transformation (move, rotate, and scale) and you can duplicate them to have multiple collisions. Click on the collision shape inside static mesh editor and you can switch between move, rotate, and scale using *W*, *E*, and *R*. You can use *Alt* + left click drag (or *Ctrl* + *W*) to duplicate an existing collision.

Materials

Unreal Engine can import materials and textures to apply to the mesh while exporting from 3D application. From Autodesk 3ds Max, only the basic materials are supported. They are **Standard** and **Multi/Sub-Object**. In those basic materials, only specific features are supported. This means FBX will not export all settings but it supports certain maps or textures used in that material type.

In the following example, you can see a model with multiple materials assigned.

Note that it is very important to have unique names for each sub material in the **Multi/Sub-Object** material. Each sub material has a unique name as shown in the following screenshot:

LOD

Level of Detail (LOD) is a way to limit the impact of meshes as they get farther away from the camera. Each LOD will have reduced triangles and vertices compared to the previous one and can have simpler materials. That means base LOD (**LOD 0**) will be the high quality mesh that appears when the player is near. As the player goes farther from that object, it will change to **LOD 1** with reduced triangles and vertices than **LOD 0** and as the player goes even farther away it will switch to **LOD 2**, which has much fewer triangles and vertices than **LOD 1**.

The following figure should give you an idea about what LOD does. The mesh on the left is base LOD (**LOD 0**), the middle is **LOD 1**, and the right is **LOD 2**.

 More information about LODs can be found at `https://docs.` `unrealengine.com/latest/INT/Engine/Content/Types/` `StaticMeshes/HowTo/LODs/index.html`.

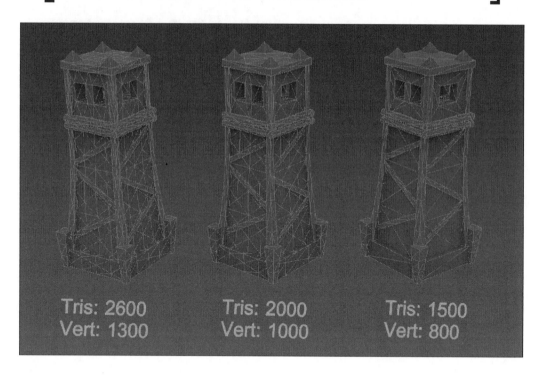

Exporting and importing

We will now cover how to export and import a mesh into Unreal.

Exporting

Exporting a mesh is a pretty straightforward process. You can export multiple meshes in a single FBX file or export each mesh individually. Unreal importer can import multiple meshes as separate assets or combine them as a single asset by enabling the **Combine Meshes** option at import time.

In the following screenshot, you can see that I have selected both the collision mesh and the model for exporting:

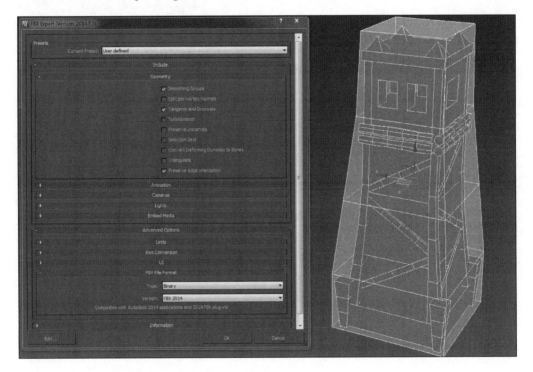

 Smoothing Groups should be turned on when exporting, otherwise Unreal Engine will show a warning when importing.

Importing

Importing a mesh into Unreal is simple. There are three ways you can import. They are explained here.

Context menu

You can right-click inside **Content Browser** and select **Import to <Your folder name>**.

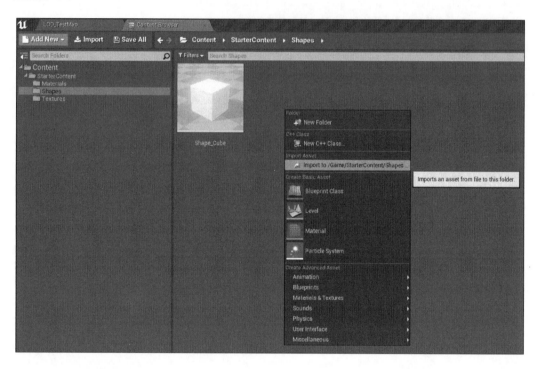

Drag and drop

As the name states, you can easily drag a FBX or OBJ model from **Windows Explorer** to **Content Browser** to import.

Content Browser import

Content Browser has an **Import** button that you can use to import meshes.

Automatic import

If you place FBX files in your project's **Content** folder (including any subfolders), Unreal will automatically detect this and trigger the import process (if you have the editor open. Otherwise, the next time you run it).

Configuring automatic import

You can choose whether you want this option enabled or disabled. To configure, go to **Edit | Editor Preferences | Loading & Saving | Auto Reimport**.

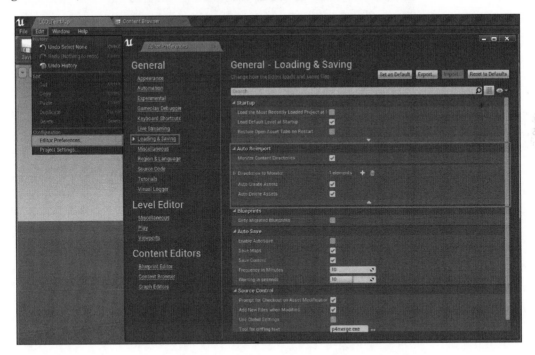

- **Monitor Content Directories**: This enables or disables automatic importing of assets.

- **Directories to Monitor**: This adds or removes a path (it can be a virtual package path such as \Game\MyContent\ or an absolute path such as C:\My Contents) for the engine to monitor new content.

- **Auto Create Assets**: If enabled, any new FBX files will not be automatically imported.

- **Auto Delete Assets**: If enabled, and you delete the FBX file from Explorer, Unreal Engine will prompt whether you want to delete the asset file as well.

Result

When you import your asset, you will see the **Import Options** dialog. You can read all about the import settings here:

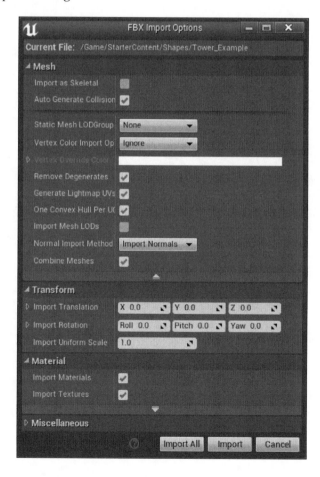

Once you click on **Import** (or **Import All** if you're importing multiple FBX files) you will see the asset in **Content Browser**. In the following screenshot, see how Unreal automatically imported the material from Autodesk 3ds Max:

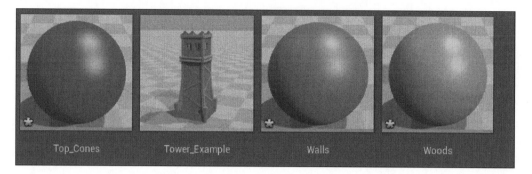

If you double-click on the static mesh (**Tower_Example**), you will see the static mesh editor. In the following screenshot, you can see that Unreal successfully imported my custom collision shape too.

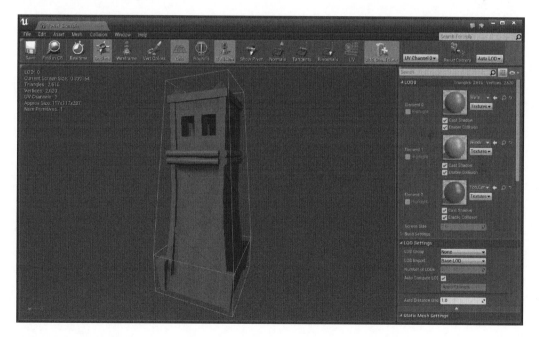

Summary

In the next chapter, you will learn more about **Materials** and **Textures**.

3
Materials

Material is an asset that defines the look of a mesh with various graph nodes that include images (textures) and math expressions. Since Unreal Engine 4 utilizes **Physically Based Rendering (PBR)**, creating realistic materials such as metal, concrete, bricks, and so on, can be quite easy. Materials in Unreal Engine define everything about the surface of the mesh, such as its color, shininess, bumpiness, and tessellation, and can even animate objects by manipulating the vertices! At this point you might think *Ok, Materials are only used for meshes* but, no, they are not actually limited to meshes. You use Materials for decals, post process, and light functions too.

Creating a Material is a pretty straightforward process. All you have to do is right-click in **Content Browser**, select **Material**, and give it a name. Done!

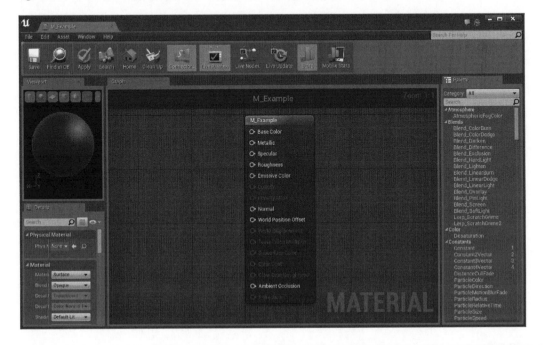

Material user interface

Now that we know what a Material is and what it does, let's take a look at the user interface of Material graph.

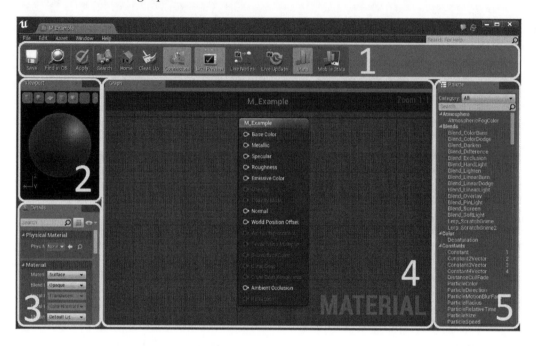

Toolbar

The **Toolbar** panel contains various buttons that help to preview graph nodes, remove isolated nodes, Material stats, and so on. Let's take a look at what these buttons do:

- **Save**: Applies the changes you made to the Material and saves the asset

- **Find in CB**: Navigates and selects this Material in **Content Browser**

- **Apply**: Applies the changes to the Material. Note that this will not save the Material

- **Search**: Searches for Material expressions or comments

- **Home**: Navigates to and selects the main canvas node

- **Clean Up**: Removes unconnected nodes

- **Connectors**: Shows or hides unconnected pins

- **Live Preview**: Toggles a real-time update of preview material

- **Live Nodes**: Toggles a real-time update of graph nodes

- **Live Update**: Recompiles a shader for every node in the graph

- **Stats**: Toggles Material stats and compilation errors
- **Mobile Stats**: Same as stats but for mobile

Live nodes might be confusing for new users so I'll explain about them further.

Live preview

Sometimes we need to preview the result of a specific node before connecting it to the main node or for debugging purposes.

To preview a node you need to right-click on the node and select **Start Previewing Node**.

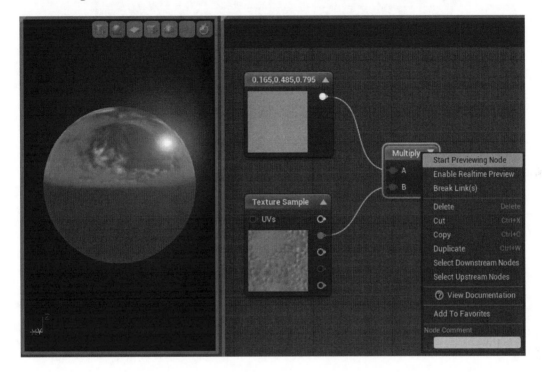

Unless you enable **Live Preview**, you will not see any changes in the preview material.

 You can press the spacebar to force a preview.

Live nodes

This will show a real-time update of nodes due to changes made by expressions to that node. See the following example:

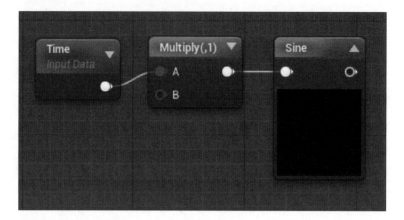

In the preceding screenshot, the **Sine** node is getting a constant update from **Time**, multiplied by one. If you enable **Live Nodes**, you will see the **Sine** node pulsing between black and white. If you change the **Multiply** value from **1** to anything else (for example, **5**) you will not see the changes unless you enable **Live Update** too.

Live update

When enabled, all expressions are compiled whenever you make a change, such as adding a new node, deleting a node, changing a property, and so on. If you have a complex graph, it is recommended to disable this option as it has to compile all nodes every time you make a change.

Preview panel

The **Preview** panel shows the result of the Material that you are currently editing. You can navigate in preview Material using these options:

- **Rotate the mesh**: Drag with the left mouse button
- **Pan**: Drag with the middle mouse button
- **Zoom**: Drag with the right mouse button
- **Update light**: Hold *L* and drag with the left mouse button

In the top-right corner of the preview viewport you can change some settings. This changes the preview mesh to the selected primitive shape:

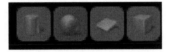

This changes the preview mesh to a custom mesh. You need to select a **Static Mesh** in **Content Browser**:

This toggles the rendering of the grid in the preview viewport:

This toggles real-time rendering in the preview viewport:

Details panel

The **Details** panel shows all the properties you can edit when you select a node in the graph. If no nodes are selected, it will show the properties of the Material itself.

For more information on these settings, please visit the Material properties documentation at `https://docs.unrealengine.com/latest/INT/Engine/Rendering/Materials/MaterialProperties/index.html`.

Graph panel

This is the main area where you create all the nodes that decide how the Material should look and behave. By default, a Material graph contains one master node that has a series of inputs, and this master node cannot be deleted. Some of the inputs are grayed out and can be enabled by changing the **Blend** mode in the **Details** panel.

Palette panel

The **Palette** panel lists all the graph nodes and Material functions that can be placed in the graph using drag and drop.

 Using the **Category** option, you can filter **Palette** contents between expressions or Material functions.

Common material expressions

There are some common Material nodes that we use most of the time when we create a material. To create a node you need to right-click on the graph canvas and search for it, or you can use the **Palette** window to drag and drop. Some nodes also have shortcut keys assigned to them.

Let's take a look at these common nodes.

Constant

Constant expression outputs a single float value and can be connected to almost any input. You can convert a constant expression to a parameter and make real-time changes to the Material instance. You can also access a parameter through Blueprint or C++ and see the changes in the game.

- **Shortcut key**: Hold *1* and click on the graph area
- **Parameter shortcut key**: Hold *S* and click on the graph area
- **Example usage**: Brighten or darken a texture

[Constant parameter is called a scalar parameter]

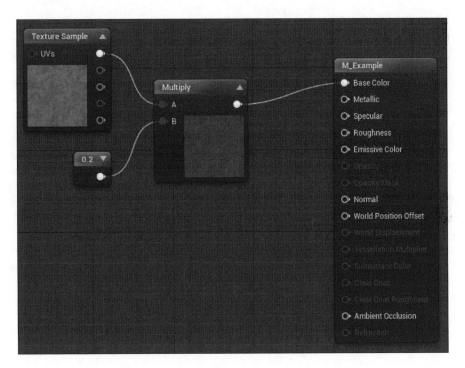

You can see a constant expression (0.2) being used to darken a texture.

Constant2Vector

The Constant2Vector expression outputs two float values, which is a two-channel vector value (for example, red channel and green channel). You can convert Constant2Vector to a parameter and make real-time changes to the Material instance or access it in Blueprint or C++ to make dynamic changes to the material while playing the game.

- **Shortcut key**: Hold 2 and click on the graph area

- **Parameter shortcut key**: Hold *V* and click on the graph area

- **Example usage**: Adjust the UVs of a texture separately

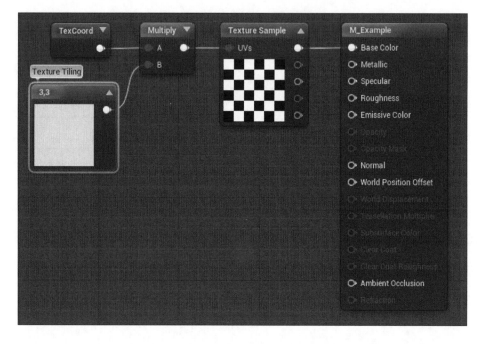

You can see a Constant2Vector being used to tile a texture in the preceding screenshot.

Constant3Vector

The Constant3Vector expression outputs three float values, which is a three-channel vector value (for example, red channel, green channel, and blue channel). You can convert Constant3Vector to a parameter and make real-time changes to a Material instance or access it in Blueprint or C++ to make dynamic changes to a material while playing the game.

- **Shortcut key**: Hold 3 and click on the graph area
- **Parameter shortcut key**: Hold *V* and click on the graph area
- **Example usage**: Change the color of a given texture

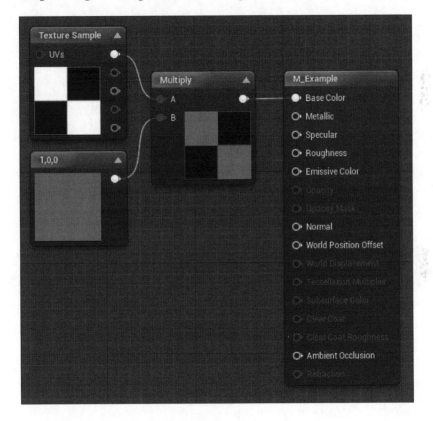

You can see Constant3Vector being used to color a grayscale texture in the preceding screenshot.

Texture coordinate (TexCoord)

The texture coordinate expression outputs texture UV coordinates as a two-channel vector (for example, U and V), which helps with tiling and also allows you to use different UV coordinates.

- **Shortcut key**: Hold *U* and click on the graph area

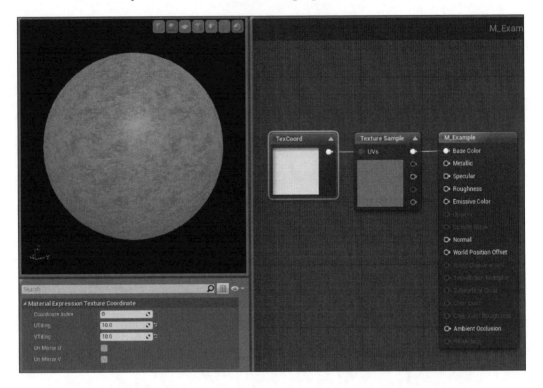

The preceding screenshot shows a texture coordinate being used to tile a texture. You can see the values used by looking at the **Details** panel in the bottom left corner.

Multiply

This expression multiplies the given inputs and outputs the result:

- Multiplication happens per channel. For example, if you multiply two vectors (0.2, 0.3, 0.4) and (0.5, 0.6, 0.7), the actual process is the following:

```
0.2 x 0.5 = 0.1
0.3 x 0.6 = 0.18
0.4 x 0.7 = 0.28
```

So the output is as follows:

```
(0.1, 0.18, 0.28)
```

- The **Multiply** node expects inputs to be the same type unless one of them is constant. In short, you cannot multiply Constant2Vector and Constant3Vector, but you can multiply Constant2Vector or Constant3Vector by a constant expression.

    ○ **Shortcut key**: Hold *M* and click on the graph area

The preceding screenshot shows a multiply node being used to boost an emissive effect.

Add

This expression adds the given inputs and outputs the result:

Addition happens per channel. For example, if you add two vectors (1, 0, 0) and (0, 1, 0), the actual process is the following:

```
1 + 0 = 1
0 + 1 = 1
0 + 0 = 0
```

So the output is as follows:

```
(1, 1, 0)
```

The **Add** node expects inputs to be the same type unless one of them is constant. In short, you cannot add Constant2Vector and Constant3Vector, but you can add Constant2Vector or Constant3Vector to a constant expression. Let's take a look at why it is like this. See the following screenshot:

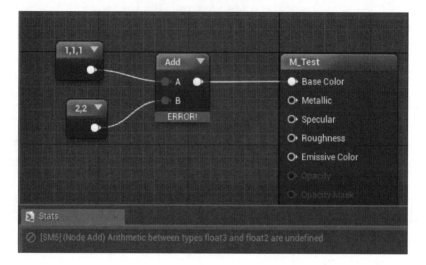

Here we are trying to add Constant3Vector and Constant2Vector but it will not work. This is because, when the Material editor tries to compile the **Add** node, it fails since the last element of Constant3Vector has nothing to add to. It will be like the following calculation:

```
1 + 2 = 3
1 + 2 = 3
1 + ? = fail
```

But you can add Constant3Vector to a constant expression, as in the following figure:

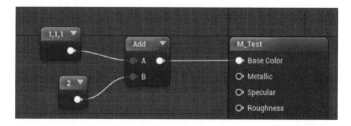

The result will be as follows:

```
1 + 2 = 3
1 + 2 = 3
1 + 2 = 3
```

And that will compile fine.

- **Shortcut key**: Hold *A* and click on the graph area

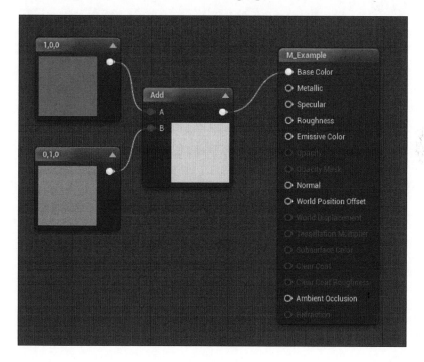

Divide

The divide expression divides the given inputs and outputs the result:

Division happens by channel. For example, if you divide two vectors (0.2, 0.3, 0.4) and (0.5, 0.6, 0.7), the actual process is like this:

```
0.2 / 0.5 = 0.4
0.3 / 0.6 = 0.5
0.4 / 0.7 = 0.571
```

So the output is as follows:

```
(0.4, 0.5, 0.571)
```

The **Divide** node expects inputs to be the same type unless one of them is constant. In short, you cannot divide Constant2Vector by Constant3Vector, but you can divide Constant2Vector or Constant3Vector by a constant expression.

- **Shortcut key**: Hold *D* and click in the graph area

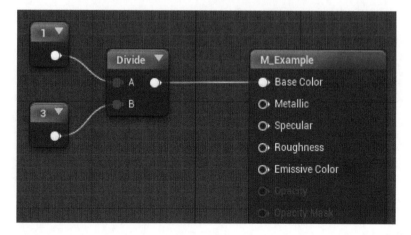

Subtract

This expression subtracts the given inputs and outputs the result:

Subtraction happens by channel. For example, if you subtract two vectors (0.2, 0.3, 0.4) and (0.5, 0.6, 0.7), the actual process is the following:

```
0.2 - 0.5 = -0.3
0.3 - 0.6 = -0.3
0.4 - 0.7 = -0.3
```

So the output is as follows:

```
(-0.3, -0.3, -0.3)
```

The **Subtract** node expects inputs to be the same type unless one of them is constant. In short, you cannot subtract Constant2Vector from Constant3Vector, but you can subtract Constant2Vector or Constant3Vector from a constant expression.

- **Shortcut key**: No shortcut key

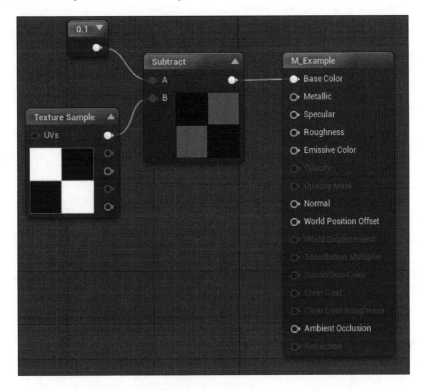

Texture sample (Texture2D)

Texture sample outputs the given texture. It also outputs all four channels (namely, red, green, blue, and alpha) from the texture separately so you can use them for various things. This is especially useful if you work on multiple grayscale textures (such as mask textures, roughness textures, and so on). Instead of importing multiple textures, you can just create one texture in Photoshop and assign other textures to different channels and, in Material editor, you can get each channel and do all the fancy things. Oh, and did I mention Texture2D can use movie textures too?

You can convert **Texture Sample** to **TextureSampleParameter2D** and change textures in real-time via Material instance. You can also change textures dynamically in the game through Blueprints or C++.

- **Shortcut key**: Hold *T* and click in the graph area
- **Parameter shortcut key**: No shortcut key

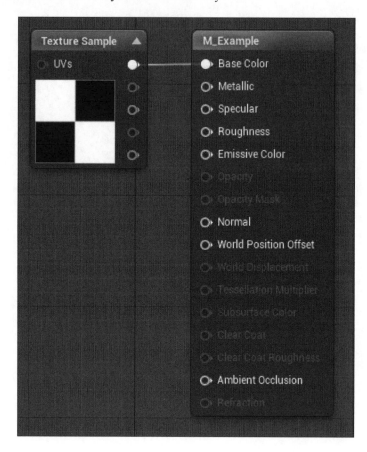

Component mask

The component mask expression can extract different channels from the input, which should be a vector channel such as **Constant2Vector**, **Constant3Vector**, **Constant4Vector**, **TextureSample**, and so on. For example, you know Constant4Vector has only one output, which is RGBA. So, if you want the green channel from RGBA, you use a component mask. You can right-click on a component **Mask** and convert it into a **Parameter** and make real-time changes in Material instance.

- **Shortcut key**: No shortcut key
- **Parameter shortcut key**: No shortcut key

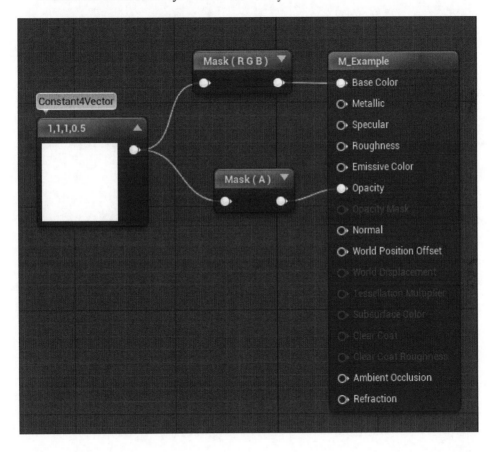

In this screenshot, we extract the alpha channel and plug it into **Opacity** and plug the RGB channel into **Base Color**.

Linear interpolate (lerp)

This blends two textures or values based on alpha. When the alpha value is **0** (black color), **A** input is used. If the alpha value is **1** (white color), **B** input is used. Most of the time, this is used to blend two textures based on a mask texture.

- **Shortcut key**: Hold *L* and click in the graph area
- **Example usage**: Blend two textures based on the alpha value, which can be a constant or a mask texture

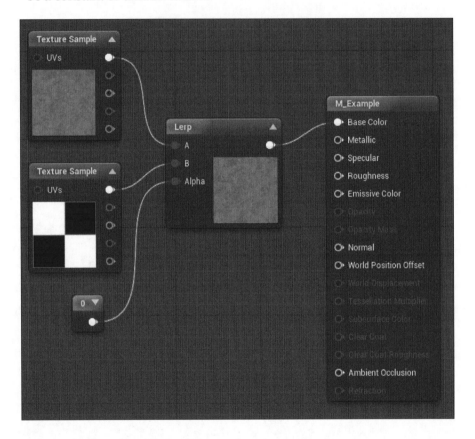

Here, the lerp node is outputting 100% of input **A** because the alpha value is **0**. If we set the alpha value to **1** then we'll see 100% of **B**. If alpha is **0.5** then we'll see a blend of both **A** and **B**.

Power

The **Power** node multiplies the base input by itself with Exp times. For example, if you have **4** in **Base** and **6** in **Exp** then the actual process is like this:

```
4 x 4 x 4 x 4 x 4 x 4 = 4096
```

So the result of **Power** is 4096.

If you apply a **Texture** to **Base** input and have a constant value (for example, **4**) then the **Texture** is multiplied four times.

- **Shortcut key**: Hold *E* and click in the graph area
- **Example usage**: Adjust the contrast of the height map or ambient occlusion map

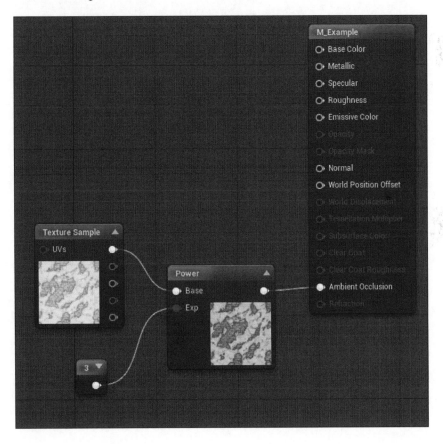

The preceding image shows a Power node being used to boost the contrast of a **Texture Sample**.

PixelDepth

PixelDepth outputs the distance to the camera of the pixel currently being rendered. This can be useful to alter the appearance of the material based on the distance from the player.

- **Shortcut key**: No shortcut key
- **Example usage**: Change the color of an object based on the distance from the player

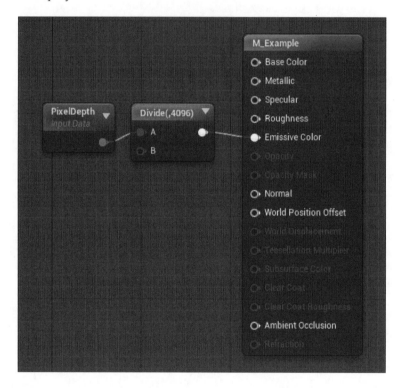

If you apply the previous material to a mesh, then the color of the mesh will be changed based on the distance to the player camera.

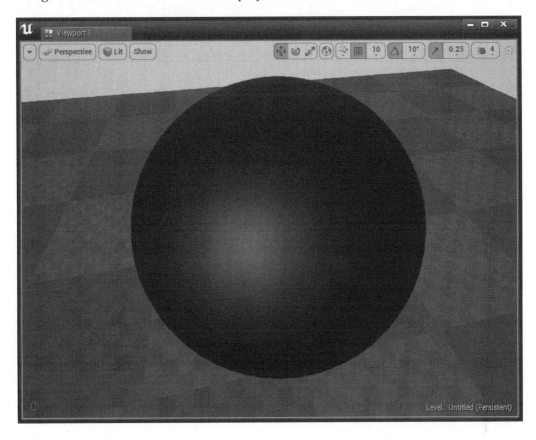

The preceding screenshot shows how the mesh will look closer to the player camera.

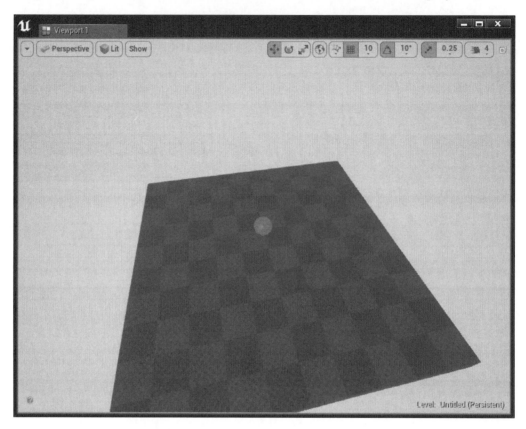

The preceding screenshot shows how the mesh will look when it's farther away from the player camera.

Desaturation

As the title says, the **Desaturation** expression desaturates its input. Simply put, it can convert a color image to grayscale based on a certain percentage.

- **Shortcut key**: No shortcut key

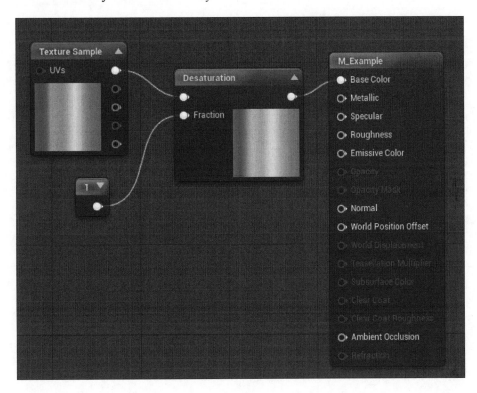

Time

This expression outputs the **Time** passage of the game (in seconds). This is used if you want your Material to change over time.

- **Shortcut key**: No shortcut key
- **Example usage**: Create a pulsing Material

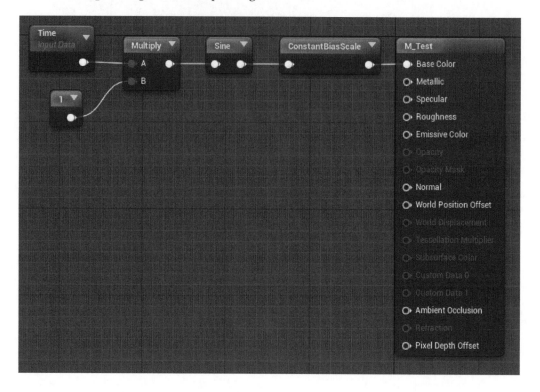

In the previous material, we multiply **Time** by a constant expression. The result of the **Multiply** node is plugged into the **Sine** node, which outputs a continuous oscillating waveform that outputs the value in a range of **-1** to **1**. We then use a **ConstantBiasScale** node to prevent the value from going below **0**. A **ConstantBiasScale** node is basically a node that adds a bias value to the input and multiplies it by a scale value. By default, bias is set to **0.5** and scale to **1**. So if the **Sine** value is **-1**, then the result is `(-1 + 1) * 0.5`, which equals **0**.

Fresnel

Fresnel creates rim lighting, which means it will highlight the edges of the mesh.

• **Shortcut key**: No shortcut key

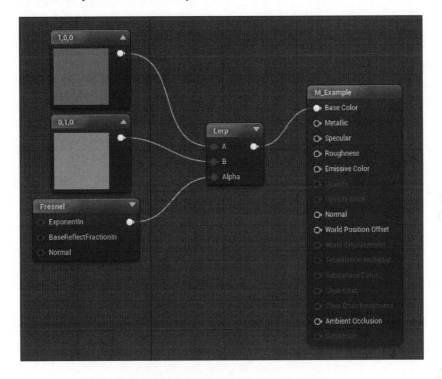

The result of the previous network is as follows:

Material types

Now that you know some of the basic expressions, let's take a look at different Material types. First of all, obviously, is the main Material editor, but then you also have Material instances, Material functions, and layered Materials.

Material instances

Material instance is used to change the appearance of a Material without recompiling it. When you change any value in Material editor and apply it, it will recompile the whole shader and create a set of shaders. When you create a Material instance from that Material, it will use the same set of shaders so you can change the values in real time without recompiling anything. But when you use **Static Switch Parameter** or **Component Mask Parameter** in your **Parent Material**, then it's different because each of those parameters has unique combinations. For example, let's say you have **Material_1** with no **Static Switch Parameter**, and **Material_2** with **Static Switch Parameter** called **bEnableSwitch**. **Material_1** will create only one set of shaders, while **Material_2** will create two sets of shaders with **bEnableSwitch = False** and **bEnableSwitch = True**.

An example workflow is to create a master Material that contains all the necessary parameters and let the designers make different versions.

There are two types of Material instances. They are:

- Material Instance Constant
- Material Instance Dynamic

Only Material Instance Constant has a user interface. Material Instance Dynamic has no user interface and cannot be created in content browser.

Material Instance Constant

As the title says, **Material Instant Constant (MIC)** is only editable in the editor. That means you cannot change the values at runtime. MIC exposes all parameters you created in the parent Material. You can create your own groups and organize all your parameters nicely.

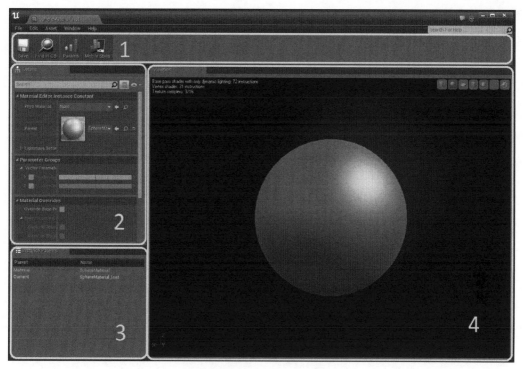

Material Instance User Interface

- **Toolbar (1)**: The following are toolbar options:
  - ° **Save**: Saves the asset
  - ° **Find in CB**: Navigates to this asset in Content Browser and selects it
  - ° **Params**: Exposes all parameters from Parent Material
  - ° **Mobile Stats**: Toggles Material stats for Mobile

- **Details (2)**: Displays all the parameters from parent Material and other properties of Material instance. Here you can also assign a physics Material and override the base properties of the parent Material, such as blend mode, two-sided, and so on.

- **Instance parents (3)**: Here you will see a chain of parents all the way up to the main master Material. The instance currently being edited is shown in bold.

- **Viewport (4)**: The viewport displays the material on a mesh so you can see your changes in real time. You can change the preview shape in the top-right corner. This is the same as it was in Material editor.

Material Instance Constant example

In order for Material instance to work, we need a master Material with parameters. Let's create a simple Material that will change its color based on the distance to the player, that is, when the player is near the mesh it will have a red color, and as they move further away it will change its color. Note that there are 21 parameter expressions in UE4.

Right now we will stick with two common parameters, and they are as follows:

- Scalar parameter
- Vector parameter

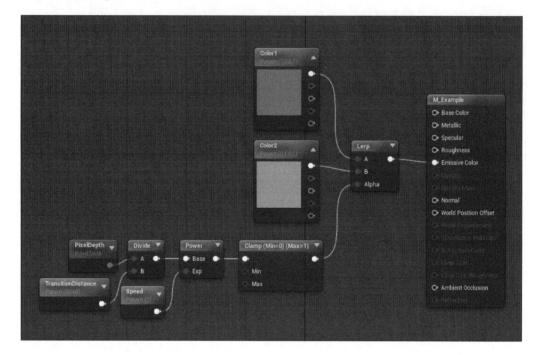

As you can see in the previous screenshot, we created two vector parameters (**Color1**, **Color2**) and two scalar parameters (**TransitionDistance**, **Speed**). We will use these parameters to modify in real time. To create an instance of this Material you need to right-click on this Material in **Content Browser** and select **Create Material Instance**. This will create a new instance Material right next to this Material.

If you open that instance you will see all these parameters there, and you can edit them in real time without having to wait for the Material to recompile:

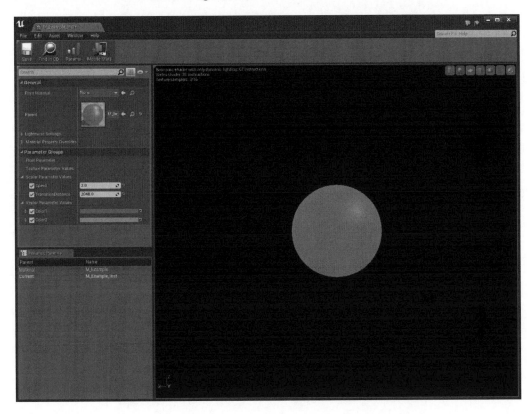

To change values in Material instance, you need to override them first. You need to click the checkbox near the parameter to override the values. As shown in the following screenshot:

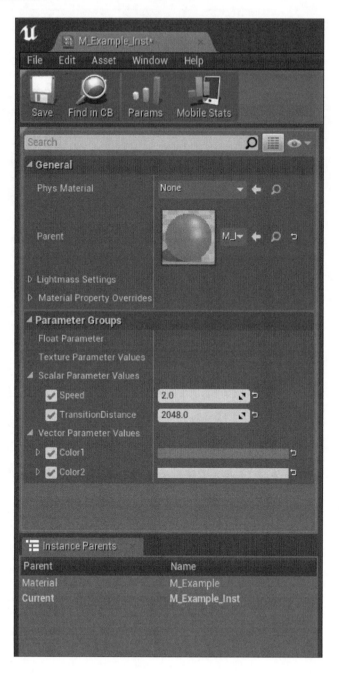

Material functions

Material functions are graphs that contain a set of nodes that can be used across any number of Materials. If you often find yourself creating complex networks then it's better to make a Material function so you can contain all these complex networks in one single node. One thing to keep in mind is that Material function cannot contain any parameter nodes (for example, **Scalar Parameter**, **Vector Parameter**, **Texture Parameter**, and so on). To pass data into a Material function, you need to use a special **FunctionInput** node. Similarly, if you want data out of a Material function, you need to use the **FunctionOutput** node. By default, Material function creates one output for you but you can create more outputs if you want.

The UI of Material function is almost the same as of Material editor. If you check the **Details** panel you will see some options to help you get the most out of your Material function. Let's take a look at these options:

- **Description**: This appears as a tooltip when you hover the mouse on this function node in Material graph.

- **Expose to Library**: Enable this to show your Material function when you right-click inside your Material graph.

- **Library Categories**: This list the categories this function belongs to. By default, it belongs to the **Misc** category but you can change it and add as many categories as you want.

[Material functions cannot be applied surface, so if you want to use a Material function you must use it in a Material.]

Material function example

To create a Material function, first right-click in **Content Browser** and go to **Materials & Textures** and select **Material Function**. In this example, we will create a Material function called **Normal Map Adjuster** that can boost the intensity of a normal map. Let's see what we need to create such a function:

- **Texture [INPUT]**: Obviously we need to pass a texture that needs to be modified.

- **Intensity [INPUT]**: We also need to pass how intense the normal should be. A value of **0** means no changes to the normal map and a value of **1** means a boosted normal effect.

- **Result [OUTPUT]**: Finally we will output the result, which we can connect to the normal channel in our Material.

The final output node (result) can be renamed with any custom name you want. Select the node and, in the **Details** panel, change **Output Name**.

Open your Material function and right-click on the graph and search for **Input**.

Select the **FunctionInput** node. You will see some properties in the **Details** panel for the **Input** node you just selected.

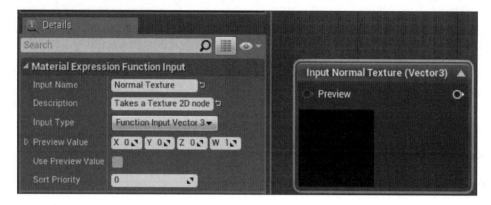

Let's take a look at these settings:

- **Input Name**: A custom name for the input. You can name it whatever you want. Here, I called it **Normal Texture**.

- **Description**: Will be used as a tooltip when you hover over this input in Material graph.

- **Input Type**: Defines the type of input for this node.

- **Preview Value**: Value to use if this input is not connected in Material graph. Only used if **Use Preview Value as Default** is checked.

- **Use Preview Value as Default**: If checked, it will use the **Preview Value** and will mark this input as optional. So when you use this function, you can leave this input unconnected. But if you disable this option, then you must connect the required node to this when in Material graph.

- **Sort Priority**: Arranges this input in relation to other input nodes.

Let's create a simple network to boost the normal effect. Take a look at the following screenshot:

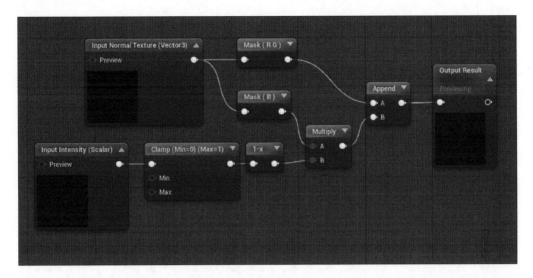

Here we are extracting the red, green, and blue channels separately. The reason behind this is simply that we need to multiply **Intensity** (scalar input value) by only the blue channel to increase the normal effect. The **Intensity** needs to be clamped between **0** and **1** and then inverted using the **1-x** (OneMinus) node because, when we use this Material function in a Material, we need **0** to have the default normal intensity and **1** to really boost the effect. Without the OneMinus node it will be the opposite, that is, **0** will boost the normal map effect and **1** will have a regular effect.

Now that the function is done, click the **Save** button on the toolbar.

 Saving automatically compiles the Material.

Now to get this into Material, right-click inside the Material graph and search for **NormalMapAdjuster**. Then all you have to do is plug a **Normal** map and a **Scalar Parameter** to **NormalMapAdjuster** and connect it to the **Normal** channel.

 If it doesn't show up in the context menu, make sure you enabled **Expose to Library** in Material Function.

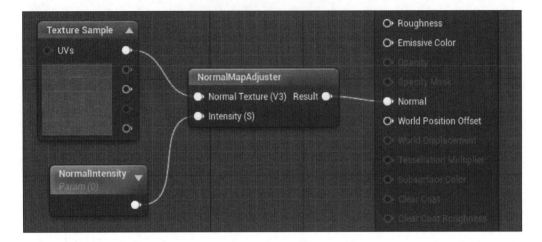

In your Material instance you can adjust **NormalIntensity** in real time.

Layered Material

Layered Materials are basically *Materials within Materials* and exist as an extension of Material function. The basic workflow is as follows: you create a **Make Material Attribute** (which features all the material attributes, such as **Base Color**, **Metallic**, **Specular**, **Roughness**, and so on) and you connect your nodes to it. Then you connect the output of **Make Material Attributes** to the input of the **Output Result** node.

Layered Materials are most beneficial when your assets have different layers of materials. For example, think about a character with different elements such as metallic armor, leather gloves, skin, and so on. Defining each of these materials and blending them in a conventional way will make the material complexity increase significantly. If you use layered Material in such cases, you can define each of those materials as a single node and blend them very easily.

Creating layered Material using make material attributes

For this example we will create two simple layered Materials and blend them together in our final material. First, create a Material function and open it. In Material function, follow these steps:

1. Right-click on the graph editor and search for **Make Material Attributes** and select the node from that menu.

2. Create a **Constant3Vector** node and connect it to **BaseColor** of **Make Material Attributes**.

3. Create a constant value and connect it to **Metallic** of **Make Material Attributes**.

4. Create one more constant value and connect that to **Roughness** of **Make Material Attributes**.

5. Finally, connect **Make Material Attributes** to the output of Material function.

The final Material function should look like this. Note the values I'm using for constant nodes.

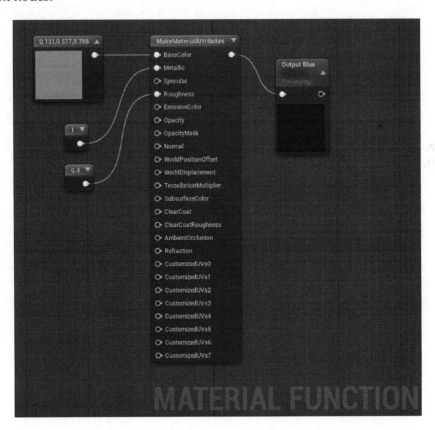

Since we want this to be **Metallic**, we set **Metallic** to **1**.

We will create a duplicate of this same Material function and make it a non-metallic Material with a different color. See the following image:

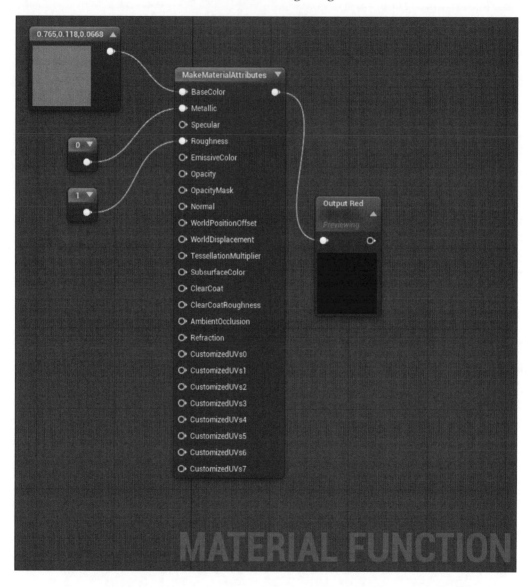

This is a non-metallic Material and we are going to blend these two Materials in our Material editor using a default **Material Layer Blend** function.

Make sure you expose both of these Material functions so we can use them in Material editor.

Open an existing Material or create a new one in **Content Browser** and open it:

1. Right-click on the graph and search for your Material functions (select both of them).

2. Right-click again on the graph and search and select **MatLayerBlend_ Simple**.

3. Connect your Material functions to **MatLayerBlend_Simple**. Connect one function to **Base Material** and the other one to **Top Material**.

4. Now, to blend these two materials we need an **Alpha (Scalar)** value. A value of **1** (white) will output **Base Material** and a value of **0** will output **Top Material**. A value of **0.5** will output a mix of both **Base** and **Top** materials.

Since we are using layered Material we cannot directly connect this to the Material editor like other nodes. To make this work, there are two ways we can connect.

Method 1:

We can make the material use Material attributes instead of regular nodes. To use this feature, click anywhere on the graph and in the **Details** panel select **Use Material Attributes**:

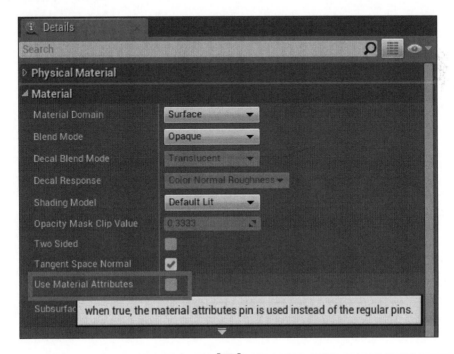

When you enable this, the main material node will show only one node called Material attributes so you can connect the output of **MatLayerBlend_Simple** to this node.

The following is a screenshot of the final material using this method:

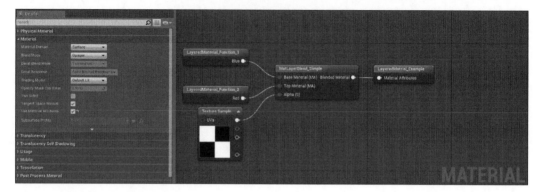

Method 2:

In this method, instead of using Material attributes for the main node we use **BreakMaterialAttributes** and connect them as regular nodes:

1. Right-click on the graph area and search and select **BreakMaterialAttributes**.

2. Connect the output of **MatLayerBlend_Simple** to **BreakMaterialAttributes**.

3. And finally, connect all the output nodes of **BreakMaterialAttributes** to the main node of Material editor.

The following is a screenshot of the final material using this method:

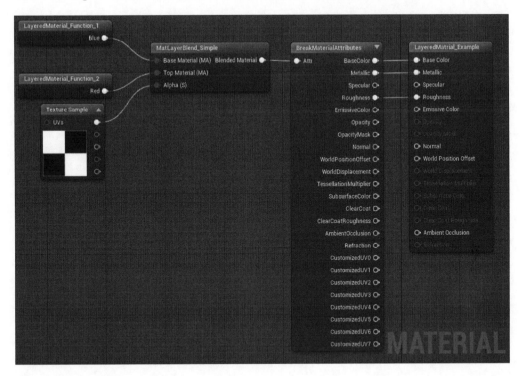

Summary

In the next chapter we will use post processing techniques to enhance the look of your scene. We will also create a simple Material and use it in post process Material.

4
Post Process

Post Process in Unreal Engine 4 allows you to create a variety of artistic effects and change the overall look and feel of the whole game. Post Process effects are activated using Post Process Volumes and can be used individually to affect only a specific area or the entire scene. You can have multiple Post Process Volumes overlapping and render their effects based on their priority. Post Process Volumes can be used to add or modify simple effects such as Bloom, Lens Flares, Eye Adaptation, Depth of Field, and so on and they can also be used to get advanced effects using Materials. Another great feature of Post Process Volume is **Look up Table (LUT)**, which is used to store color transformations from image editing software, such as Adobe Photoshop or GIMP. They are very easy to set up and can yield very good results. We will get into LUT later in this chapter.

When you first start a project without starter content, there will be no Post Process Volumes present in the scene, so Engine will use the default settings. You can change these settings per project under **Project Settings**:

1. Click on **Edit** in the menu bar.
2. Click on **Project Settings**.
3. Go to the **Rendering** section.

4. Expand **Default Postprocessing Settings**:

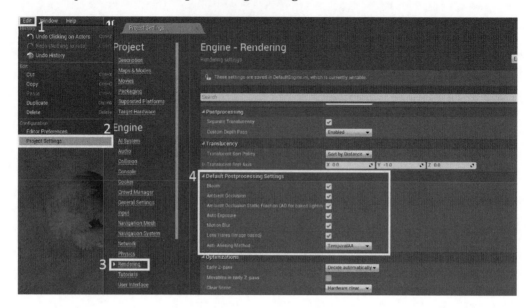

Here, you will see the default settings for Unreal Engine when there is no Post Process Volume in your scene. You can modify these settings or add a Post Process Volume to override them independently.

Adding Post Process

To use Post Process, you need a Post Process Volume in your scene:

1. Go to the **Modes** tab (if you closed it, press *Shift + 1*).
2. Select the **Volumes** tab.

3. Drag and drop Post Process Volume into the scene:

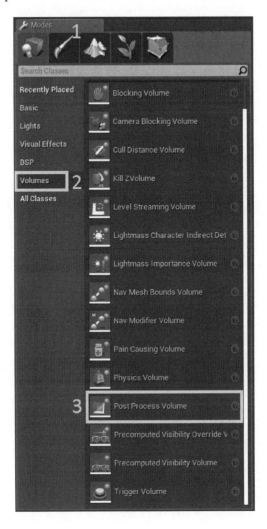

You now have a Post Process Volume in your scene. However, it only shows the effects when the player is inside that volume. To make it affect the whole scene perform the following steps:

1. Select **Post Process Volume**
2. In the **Details** panel, scroll down and expand the **Post Process Volume** section
3. Enable **Unbound**

Enabling **Unbound** will ignore the bounds of this volume and affect the whole scene. Now, let's take a quick look at these Post Process settings:

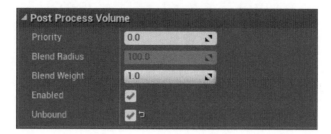

-   **Priority**: If multiple volumes are overlapping each other, then the volume with higher priority overrides the lower one.
-   **Blend Radius**: This is the radius of the volume used for blending. Generally, a value of 100 works best. This setting is ignored if you have **Unbound** enabled.
-   **Blend Weight**: This defines the influence of properties. 0 means no effect and 1 means full effect.
-   **Enabled**: This enables or disables this volume.
-   **Unbound**: If enabled, then Post Process effects will ignore the bounds of this volume and will affect the whole scene.

LUT

LUTs are color neutral textures unwrapped to a 256 x 16 size texture. They are used to create unique artistic effects and are modified using image editing software such as Adobe Photoshop. If you are not familiar with Photoshop, you can use free and open source software such as GIMP. The following is an image of the default LUT texture:

The procedure of LUT is as follows:

1. First you take a screenshot of your world and bring it into Photoshop.
2. On top of that screenshot, you insert the LUT texture.
3. Then on top of both, apply color manipulations (for example: adjustment layer).
4. Now select the LUT texture and save it with your color manipulation as PNG or TGA.
5. Finally, import your LUT into Unreal Engine.

 Note that after you import your LUT into **Content Browser**, open it and set the **Texture Group** to **ColorLookupTable**. This is an important step and should not be skipped.

To apply the LUT, select the Post Process volume, and under the **Scene Color** section, you can enable **Color Grading** and set your LUT texture:

With the **Color Grading Intensity** option, you can change the intensity of the effect.

Post Process Materials

Post Process Materials help you create custom post processing with the help of Material Editor. You need to create a Material with your desired effect and assign it to **Blendables** in Post Process Volume. Click on the plus sign to add more slots:

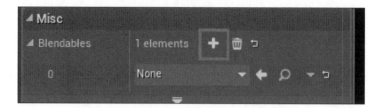

Before I explain about Post Process Materials, let's take a quick look at one of the most important Post Process nodes in Material Editor:

- **Scene Texture**: This node has multiple selections that output different textures:

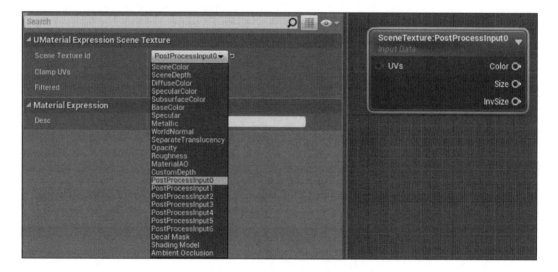

- **UVs** (optional): This input tiles the texture. For UV operations on the **SceneTexture** node, it is good to use the **ScreenPosition** node instead of the regular **Texture Coordinate** node.

- **Color**: This outputs the final texture as RGBA. If you want to multiply this with a color, you first need to use a component mask to extract R, G, and B and then multiply it by your color.

- **Size**: This outputs the size (width and height) of the texture.

- **InvSize**: This is the inverse of the **Size** output. (1/width and 1/height).

 It is important to keep in mind that you should only use Post Process Materials when you really need them. For **Color Correction** and various other effects, you should stick with the settings from Post Process Volume since they are more efficient and optimized.

Creating a Post Process Material

With Post Process Material, you can create your own custom Post Processing effects. Some examples are:

- Highlighting a specific object in your game
- Rendering occluded objects
- Edge detection, and so on

In this quick example, we will see how to highlight an object in our world. To render a specific object separately, we need to put them to a custom depth buffer. The good thing is, it's as easy as clicking on a checkbox.

Select your Static Mesh and under the **Rendering** section, expand the options and enable **Render Custom Depth**:

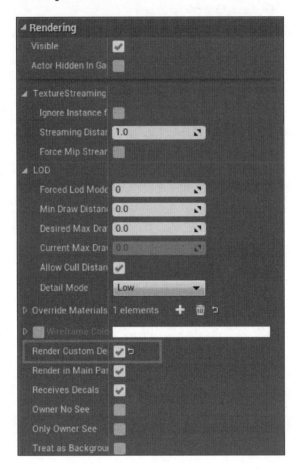

Now that the mesh is rendered in the CustomDepth buffer, we can use this information in Material Editor to mask out and render it separately. To do that:

1. Create a new Material and open it.

2. First thing to do now is to set **Material Domain** to **Post Process**. This will disable all inputs except **Emissive Color**.

3. Now, right-click on the graph and search for **SceneTexture** and select it. Set **Scene Texture Id** to **CustomDepth**.

4. **CustomDepth** outputs a raw value so let's divide it by the distance we want.

5. Add a new **Divide** node and connect **CustomDepth** to input *A*. Select the divide node and for *Const B* give a high value (for example: 100000000). Remember, 1 Unreal Unit is equal to 1 cm so if you give a small value like 100 or 1000, you need to go really close to the object to see the effect. This is why we use a very large value.

6. Add a **Clamp** node and connect **Divide** to the first input of the **Clamp** node.

7. Create a **Lerp** node and connect the output of **Clamp** to the *Alpha* input of **Lerp**. The **Lerp** node will blend input A and B based on the alpha value. If the alpha value is 1, then input *A* is used. If it is 0 then input *B* is used.

8. Create another **SceneTexture** node and set its *Scene Texture Id* to **PostProcessInput0**. **PostProcessInput0** outputs the final HDR color so make sure you use this. There's another output called **SceneColor**, which does the same but it outputs lower quality of the current scene.

9. Right-click on the graph again and search for the **Desaturation** node. Connect **PostProcessInput0** *Color* output to **Desaturation** input. We will use this to desaturate the whole scene except our mesh with **CustomDepth**.

10. Connect the **Desaturation** output to *Lerp B* and **PostProcessInput0** to *Lerp A*, and finally, connect the **Lerp** to **Emissive Color**.

Here is the final screenshot of the whole graph:

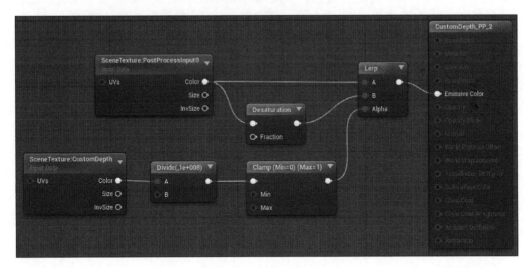

And in this example scene, I've applied this Material to Post Process Blendables and you can see the effect:

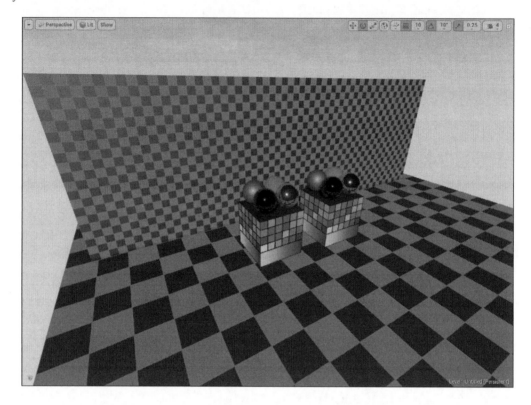

Everything that is in color has Render Custom Depth enabled so the Post Process Material is masking them out and applying the desaturation to the entire scene.

Summary

In next chapter, we will add lights and discuss Light Mobility, Lightmass, and Dynamic Lights.

5
Lights

Lighting is an important factor in your game, which can be easily overlooked, and wrong usage can severely impact on performance. But with proper settings, combined with post process, you can create very beautiful and realistic scenes.

In this chapter, we will look into different light mobilities and learn more about Lightmass Global Illumination, which is the static Global Illumination solver created by Epic games. We will also learn how to prepare assets to be used with it.

Lighting basics

In this section, we will see how to place lights and how to adjust some important values.

Placing lights

In Unreal Engine 4, lights can be placed in two different ways. Through the modes tab or by right-clicking in the level:

- **Modes tab**: In the **Modes** tab, go to the place tab (*Shift + 1*) and go to the **Lights** section. From there you can drag and drop various lights.

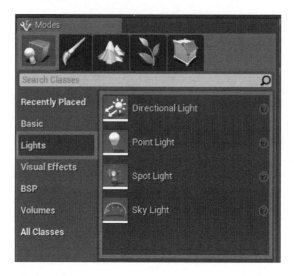

- **Right-clicking**: Right-click in viewport and in **Place Actor** you can select your light.

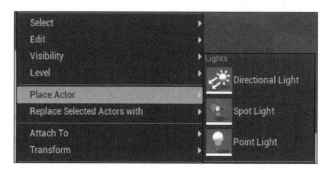

Once a light is added to the level, you can use the transform tool (*W* to move, *E* to rotate) to change the position and rotation of your selected light.

[

Since **Directional Light** casts light from an infinite source, updating their location has no effect.
]

Various lights

Unreal Engine 4 features four different types of light Actors. They are:

- **Directional Light**: Simulates light from a source that is infinitely far away. Since all shadows cast by this light will be parallel, this is the ideal choice for simulating sunlight.

- **Spot Light**: Emits light from a single point in a cone shape. There are two cones (inner cone and outer cone). Within the inner cone, light achieves full brightness and between the inner and outer cone a falloff takes place, which softens the illumination. That means after the inner cone, light slowly loses its illumination as it goes to the outer cone.

- **Point Light**: Emits light from a single point to all directions, much like a real-world light bulb.

- **Sky Light**: Does not really emit light, but instead captures the distant parts of your scene (for example, Actors that are placed beyond **Sky Distance Threshold**) and applies them as light. That means you can have lights coming from your atmosphere, distant mountains, and so on. Note that **Sky Light** will only update when you rebuild your lighting or by pressing **Recapture Scene** (in the **Details** panel with **Sky Light** selected).

Common light settings

Now that we know how to place lights into a scene, let's take a look at some of the common settings of a light. Select your light in a scene and in the **Details** panel you will see these settings:

- **Intensity**: Determines the intensity (energy) of the light. This is in lumens so, for example, 1700 lm corresponds to a 100 W bulb.

- **Light Color**: Determines the color of the light.

- **Attenuation Radius**: Sets the limit of the light. It also calculates the falloff of the light. This setting is only available in **Point Lights** and **Spot Lights**.

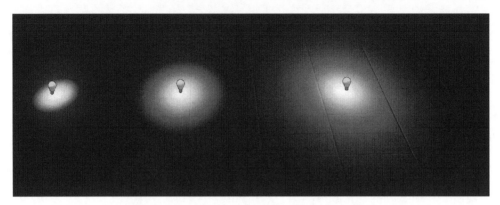

Attenuation Radius from left to right: 100, 200, 500.

- **Source Radius**: Defines the size of specular highlights on surfaces. This effect can be subdued by adjusting the **Min Roughness** setting. This also affects building light using **Lightmass**. A larger **Source Radius** will cast softer shadows. Since this is processed by **Lightmass**, it will only work on **Lights** with mobility set to **Static**.

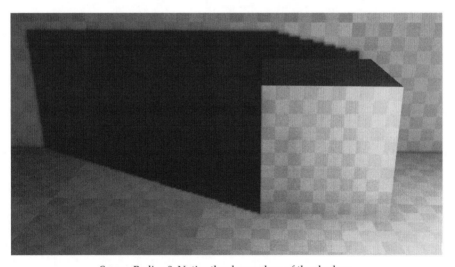

Source Radius 0. Notice the sharp edges of the shadow.

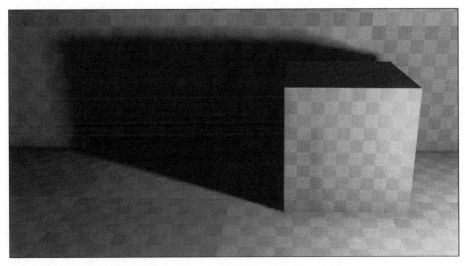

Source Radius 5. Notice the soft edges of the shadow.

- **Source Length**: Same as **Source Radius**.

Light mobility

Light mobility is an important setting to keep in mind when placing lights in your level because this changes the way light works and impacts on performance. There are three settings that you can choose. They are as follows:

- **Static**: A completely static light that has no impact on performance. This type of light will not cast shadows or specular on dynamic objects (for example, characters, movable objects, and so on). Example usage: Use this light where the player will never reach, such as distant cityscapes, ceilings, and so on. You can literally have millions of lights with static mobility.

- **Stationary**: This is a mix of static and dynamic lights and can change its color and brightness while running the game, but cannot move or rotate. Stationary lights can interact with dynamic objects and are used where the player can go.

- **Movable**: This is a completely dynamic light and all properties can be changed at runtime. Movable lights are heavier on performance so use them sparingly.

Only four or fewer stationary lights are allowed to overlap each other. If you have more than four stationary lights overlapping each other, the light icon will change to red X, which indicates that the light is using dynamic shadows at a severe performance cost!

In the following screenshot, you can easily see the overlapping light.

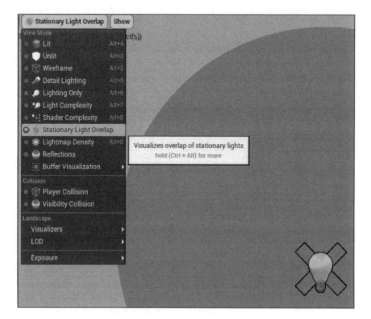

In **View** Mode, you can change to **Stationary Light Overlap** to see which light is causing an issue.

Lightmass Global Illumination

Lightmass is the high-quality static Global Illumination solver created by Epic games. **Global Illumination (GI)** means the process that simulates indirect lighting (for example, light bouncing and color bleeding from surfaces). In Unreal Engine, light bounces by default with Lightmass and is based on the base color of your material, which controls how much light should bounce from the surface of the object. Even though a more highly saturated color will bounce more light, and a less saturated color will bounce less, it all depends on the scene. In a simple room-like scene, this can be noticeable, whereas if it's an outdoor day scene this might not be that noticeable.

Let's take a quick look at the following scene:

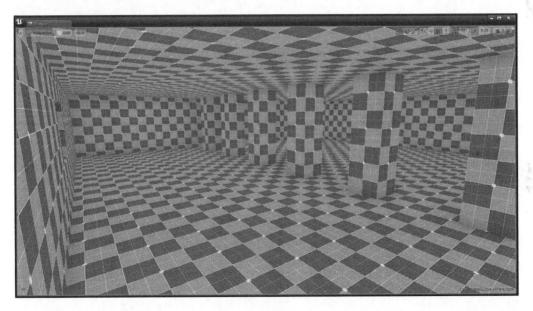

This is a simple scene in unlit mode.

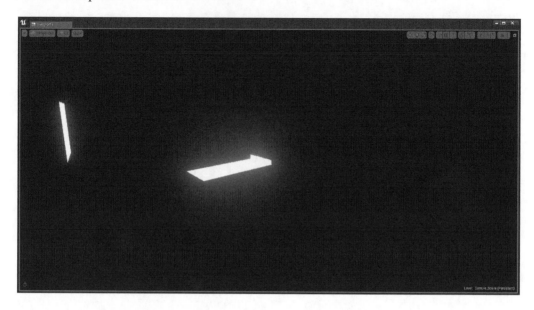

Now I added one **Directional Light** and this is how it looks with no GI.
That means there is only direct lighting and no indirect lighting (meaning there is no light bouncing).

The previous screenshot is with static GI and you can see how the whole scene came to life with GI. Notice how the pillars are casting shadows. These are called **Indirect Shadows** since they are from **Indirect Light**.

The intensity and color of indirect light depends on the light and base color of the material that the light is bouncing off. To illustrate this effect, let's take a look at the following two screenshots:

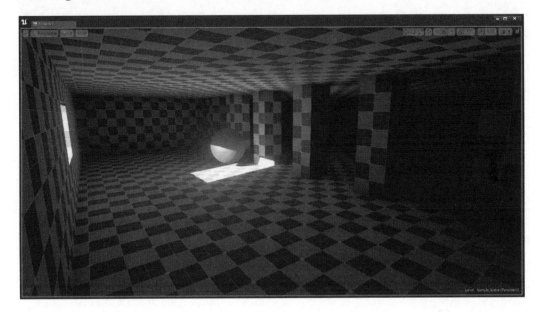

Here I applied a pure red material (the red value is 1.0) to the sphere and you can see bounced lighting picked up the base color of the red sphere changing the environment. This is called color bleeding and is most noticeable with highly saturated colors.

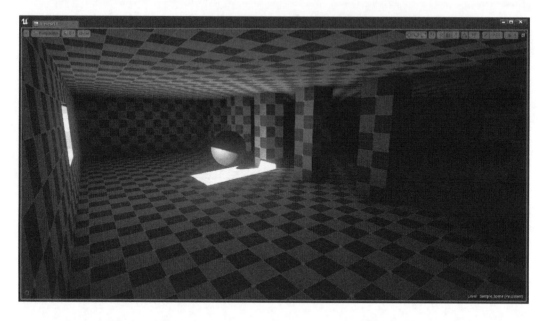

In this screenshot, I changed the value of red to 0.1 and rebuilt the lighting. And since red is more dark now, less light is bouncing. This is because darker colors will absorb the light instead of reflecting it.

Now that we know what Lightmass is, let's take a look at how we can prepare our assets to use Lightmass and learn more about Lightmass settings.

Preparing your assets for precomputed lighting

In order for your asset to have clean light and shadow details, it is necessary to have uniquely unwrapped UV to represent its own space to receive dark and light information. One rule of thumb when creating lightmap UVs is that the UV face should never overlap with any other face within the UV space. This is because if they are overlapping, then after light building, the lightmap corresponding to that space will be applied to both faces, which will result in inaccurate lighting and shadow errors. Overlapping faces are good for normal texture UVs since the texture resolution will be higher for each face, but the same rule does not apply for lightmap UVs. In a 3D program, we unwrap lightmap UVs to a new channel and use that channel in Unreal Engine 4.

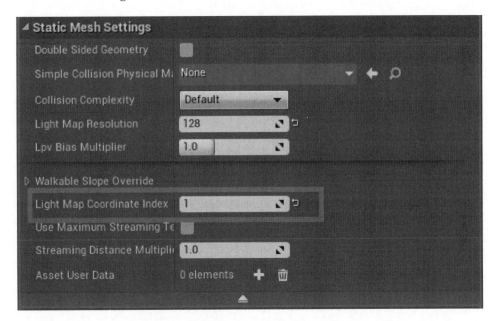

Here, you can see I'm using the second channel in my mesh for lightmap.

 Unreal starts counting from 0 while most 3d programs count from 1. That means UV channel 1 in the 3d program is UV channel 0 in Unreal, and UV channel 2 means UV channel 1 in Unreal. Here, in the previous screenshot, you can see the **Light Map Coordinate Index** is **1**, which means it is using the 2nd UV channel in mesh.

Even though you can generate lightmap UVs in Unreal Engine 4, it is highly recommended to create these UVs in a 3d program (for example, Autodesk Maya, Autodesk 3dsmax, Modo, and so on) in order to have clean lightmaps. Before creating a lightmap UV you have to set up the grid setting in your 3d app's UV editor. For example, if you have an asset that requires a lightmap resolution of 128, then your grid setting should be *1/126*, which is *0.00793650*. 128 will be the lightmap texture resolution. Higher values, such as 256, 512, 1024, and so on, will result in high-quality lightmaps but will also increase memory usage. Once we decide what lightmap resolution we need for our asset, we subtract 2 (you can also use 4) from that resolution. The reason behind this is that in order for Lightmass to calculate correctly without any filter bleeding errors, it is recommended to have a minimum of 2 pixel gaps between UVs. So if your asset is going to use a lightmap resolution of 128, it will be *128 – 2 = 126*. The reason why we divide it by 1 is that by default, Lightmass uses a 1 pixel border for filtering purposes.

Once you import your mesh into Unreal Engine 4, you set the Light Map Resolution for your Static Mesh. This value controls how good the shadow will look when another object casts a shadow onto this object.

Lightmaps are textures generated by Unreal Engine and overlayed on top of your scene. Since this is a texture, it should be in power of two (for example, 16, 32, 64, 128, 256, 512, 1024, etc.).

The floor in the preceding screenshot has a lightmap resolution of **32**. Notice inaccurate shadows on
the floor.

The floor in the preceding screenshot has a lightmap resolution of **256**. Notice better shadows on the floor.

Even though increasing the lightmap resolution gives accurate shadows, it is not a good idea to increase it for every mesh in your level as it will severely increase build times and may even crash the whole editor. For smaller objects, it is always a good idea to keep it low.

In Unreal Engine 4, you can generate lightmap UVs when importing your mesh by enabling **Generate Lightmap UVs**.

In case you miss this option, you can still generate lightmap UVs after importing. To do that perform the following steps:

1. Double-click on the **Static Mesh** in **Content Browser**.

2. Then, under the **LOD** tab, enable **Generate Lightmap UVs**.

3. Select **Source Lightmap Index**. Most of the time this will be **0** since that is normal texture UVs, and Unreal generates your lightmap UVs from texture UVs.

4. Set **Destination Lightmap Index**. This is where Unreal will save your newly created lightmap UVs. Set this to 1.

5. Click **Apply Changes** to generate lightmap UVs.

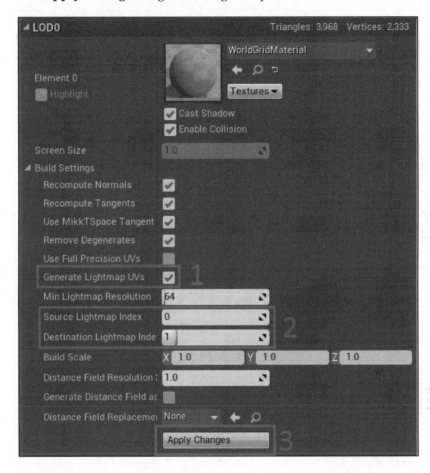

 If you already have a lightmap UV in the **Destination Lightmap Index**, it will be replaced when generating a new one.

You can preview UVs by clicking on the **UV** button in the toolbar and selecting your **UV Channel**.

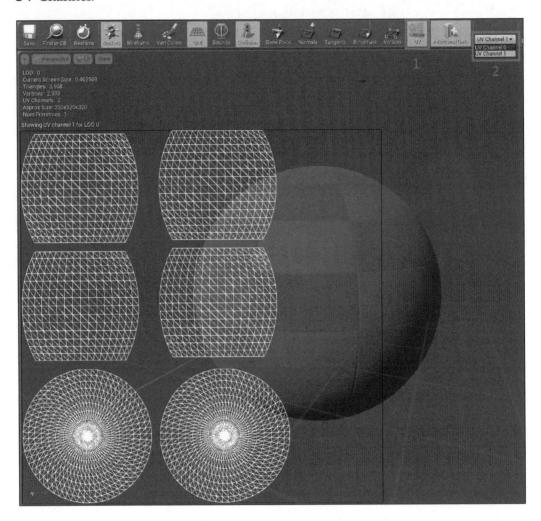

Building a scene with Lightmass

Building a scene with Lightmass is a pretty straightforward process. In order to have high-quality static Global Illumination (aka **Precomputed Lighting**), you need to have a **Lightmass Importance Volume** in your scene. This is because in many maps, we have areas large enough and the playable area is actually smaller. So instead of calculating lighting for the whole scene, which can increase light building heavily, we limit the area by using **Lightmass Importance Volume**.

Once we have a **Lightmass Importance Volume** in the scene and start light building, Lightmass will only calculate lighting within the volume. All objects outside the volume will only get one bounce of light with low quality.

To enclose the playable area in **Lightmass Importance Volume** you just have to drag and drop it from the **Modes** tab. Just like other objects, you can use transform tools (*W* to move, *E* to rotate, and *R* to scale) to adjust **Lightmass Importance Volume** in your scene. Once that is done, all you have to do is build the lighting from the **Build** button.

Alternatively, you can simply press the **Build** button, which will build the lighting. Lightmass has four different quality levels that you can choose from. They are **Preview**, **Medium**, **High**, and **Production**.

- **Preview**: Can be used while developing and this results in building the light faster.
- **Production**: When your project is near-complete or ready to ship you should use the production setting since it makes the scene more realistic and corrects various light bleed errors.

Lighting quality are just presets. There are lots of settings that should be tweaked to get the desired effect you want in your game.

Tweaking Lightmass settings

Lightmass offers a lot of options in **World Settings**, which you can tweak to get the best visual quality. You can access them by clicking on **Settings** and selecting **World Settings**.

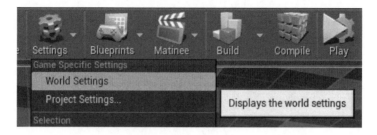

In **World Settings**, expand **Lightmass Settings** and you will see various settings you can tweak to get the most out of **Lightmass**.

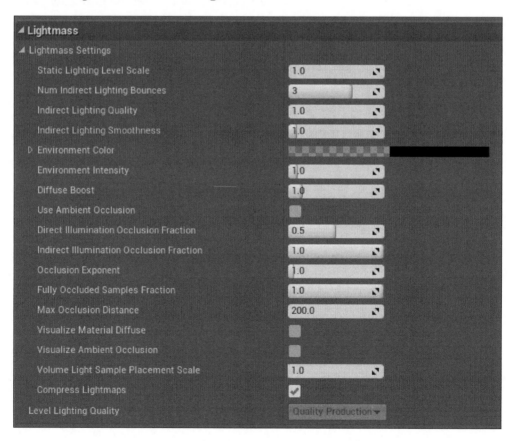

Controlling these settings helps you get the best visual quality when using Lightmass. Let's take a look at these settings:

- **Static Lighting Level**: This setting calculates the detail when building the light. Smaller values will have more detail but greatly increase build time! Larger values can be used for huge levels to lower build times.

- **Num Indirect Lighting Bounces**: This determines how many times the light should bounce off surfaces. 0 is direct lighting only, meaning there will be no Global Illumination, and 1 is one bounce of indirect lighting, and so on. Bounce 1 contributes most to the visual quality, and successive bounces are nearly free but do not add very much light since bounced light gets weaker after each bounce.

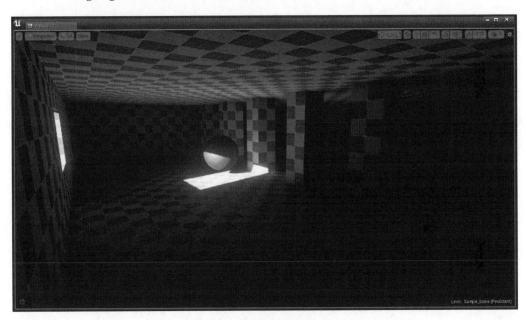

Num Indirect Lighting Bounces set to 1

- **Indirect Lighting Quality**: Higher settings result in fewer artifacts such as noise, splotchiness, and so on, but will also increase build time. Using this setting with **Indirect Lighting Smoothness** helps to get detailed indirect shadows and ambient occlusion.

- **Indirect Lighting Smoothness**: Higher values will cause Lightmass to smooth out indirect lighting but will lose detailed indirect shadows.

Indirect Lighting Quality and Smoothness set to 1.0

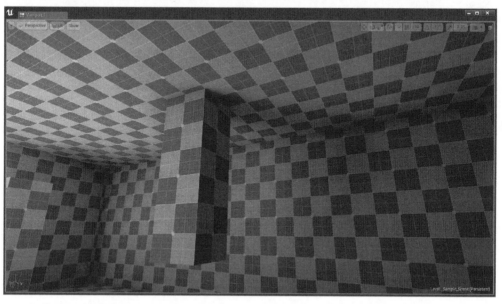

Indirect Lighting Quality: 4.0 and Indirect Lighting Smoothness: 0.5. Notice the difference in the shadow cast by the pillar

- **Environment Color**: Think of this as a big sphere surrounding the level, emitting color in all direction. That is, this acts as the HDR environment.

- **Environment Intensity**: Scales the intensity of **Environment Color**.

- **Diffuse Boost**: This is an effective way of increasing the intensity of indirect lighting in your scene. Since indirect lighting bounces off surfaces, this value will boost the influence of the color.

- **Use Ambient Occlusion**: Enables static ambient occlusion. Since ambient occlusion requires dense lighting samples, it will not look good in **Preview** builds. It's better to tweak ambient occlusion settings while you are building using production preset.

- **Direct Illumination Occlusion Fraction**: How much ambient occlusion to be applied to direct lighting.

- **Indirect Illumination Occlusion Fraction**: How much ambient occlusion to be applied to indirect lighting.

- **Occlusion Exponent**: Higher values increase the ambient occlusion contrast.

- **Fully Occluded Samples Fraction**: This value determines how much Ambient Occlusion an object should generate on other objects.

- **Max Occlusion Distance**: Maximum distance for an object to cause occlusion on another object.

- **Visualize Material Diffuse**: Overrides normal direct lighting and indirect lighting with the material diffuse term exported to Lightmass.

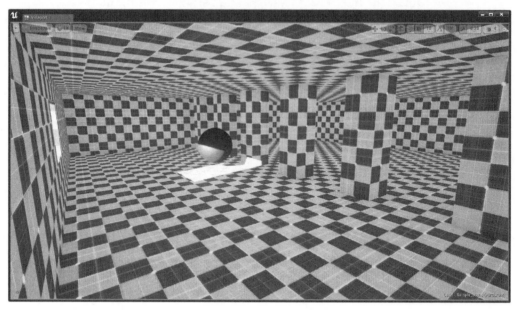

Visualize Material Diffuse enabled

- **Visualize Ambient Occlusion**: Overrides normal direct lighting and indirect lighting with ambient occlusion. This is useful when you are tweaking **Ambient Occlusion** settings.

Visualize Ambient Occlusion enabled

- **Volume Light Sample Placement Scale**: Scales the distance at which volume lighting samples are placed.

 All these Lightmass settings require lighting rebuild. So if you change any of these settings, make sure you rebuild the lighting for the changes to take effect.

Volume Light Samples are placed by Lightmass in the level after light building, and are used for dynamic objects such as characters, since Lightmass only generates lightmaps for static objects. This is also called **Indirect Lighting Cache**.

In the following screenshots, you can see how the movable object (red sphere) is lit using **Indirect Lighting Cache**:

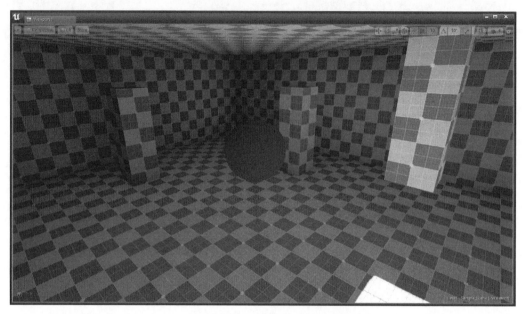

With Indirect Lighting Cache

Without Indirect Lighting Cache

Volume Light Samples are only placed within **Lightmass Importance Volume** and on static surfaces.

Indirect Lighting Cache also helps with previewing objects with unbuilt lighting. After light building, if you move a static object, it will automatically use **Indirect Lighting Cache** until the next light build.

To visualize volume lighting samples, click on **Show** | **Visualize** | **Volume Lighting Samples**.

Volume Lighting Samples previewed in the level.

You can adjust **Global Illumination Intensity** and **Color** in **Post Process Volume**. In **Post Process Volume**, expand **Post Process Settings | Global Illumination** and there you see settings for **Color** and **Intensity**.

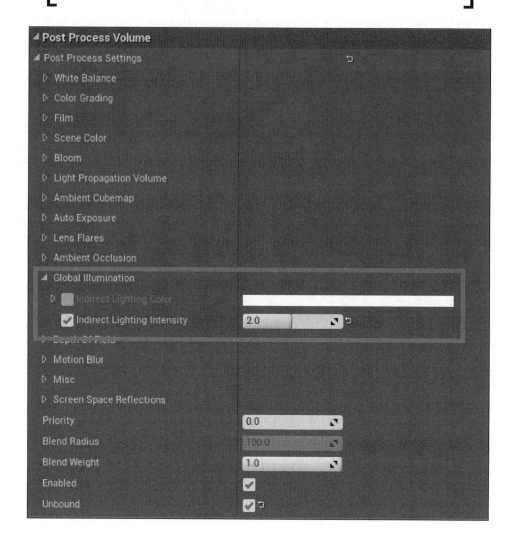

To toggle specific lighting components for debugging, you can use the various lighting component flags under the **Show | Lighting Components** section. For example, if you want to preview your scene without any direct lighting, you can turn off **Direct Lighting** and preview your scene in **Indirect Lighting** only. Keep in mind that these are only editor features and do not affect your game. These are only for debugging purposes.

Summary

In this chapter, we learned about lights and how they can improve the realism of your scene by using Lightmass Global Illumination, and how to prepare our assets to use with Lightmass. We also learned about various lights and common settings. In the next chapter we will dive into the best and most unique feature of Unreal Engine 4: Blueprints.

6
Blueprints

In this chapter, we will learn what Blueprints are and how they can be used to prototype your game. We will learn about:

- Getting familiar with Blueprint editor
- Various Blueprint graph types (for example, function graphs, event graphs, and so on)
- Blueprint nodes
- And, finally, we will create a simple Blueprint that can be placed in world or dynamically spawned while running the game

Blueprint Visual Scripting in Unreal Engine 4 is an extremely powerful and flexible node-based interface to create gameplay elements and provides artists and designers with the ability to program their game and to quickly iterate gameplay within the editor without writing a single line of code! Using Blueprints you can create and tweak gameplay, characters, inputs, environments, and virtually anything in your game.

Blueprints work by using graphs that contain various nodes connected to each other, which defines what the Blueprint does. For example, it can be gameplay events, spawning new Actors, or anything really.

Different Blueprint types

Let's take a quick look at various Blueprint types that are available in Unreal Engine 4:

- **Level Blueprint**: Level Blueprint is a special Blueprint that acts as a level-wide global event graph, which the user can neither remove nor create. Each level will have its own level Blueprint that the user can use to create events that pertain to the whole level. The user can use this graph to call events on a specific actor present in the level or play a Matinee sequence. Users who are familiar with Unreal Engine 3 (or UDK) should be familiar with this concept as this is similar to how Kismet worked in those Engines.

- **Class Blueprint**: Commonly referred to as just Blueprint, is an asset that you create inside **Content Browser**. Once the asset is created, you define its behavior visually instead of typing any code. This Blueprint is saved as an asset in **Content Browser** so you can drag and drop this into your world as an instance or spawn dynamically in another Blueprint graph.

- **Animation Blueprint**: These are specialized graphs that control the animation of a skeletal mesh by blending animations, controlling the bones directly, and outputting a final pose in each frame. Animation Blueprints will always have two graphs, namely **EventGraph** and **AnimGraph**.

- **EventGraph**: This uses a collection of animation-related events to initiate a sequence of nodes, which updates the values used to drive animations within **Animgraph**.

- **AnimGraph**: This is used to evaluate the final pose for your **Skeletal Mesh**. In this graph, you can perform animation blends or control bone transforms using **SkeletalControls**.

- **Macro Library**: These are containers that can hold various macros or graphs that you can use multiple times in any other Blueprint class. Macro libraries cannot contain variables or inherit from other Blueprints or be placed in the level. They are just a collection of graphs that you use commonly and can be a time-saver. If you are referencing a macro in your Blueprint then changes to that macro will not be applied to your Blueprint until you recompile your Blueprint. Compiling a Blueprint means converting all the properties and graphs into a class that Unreal can use.

- **Blueprint Interface**: These are graphs that contain one or more functions without implementation. Other classes that add this interface must include the functions in a unique manner. This has the same concept of interface in programming where you can access various objects with a common interface and share or send data to one another. Interface graphs have some limitations in that you cannot create variables, edit graphs, or add any components.

Getting familiar with the Blueprint user interface

The Blueprint **User Interface (UI)** contains various tabs by default. In the following screenshot you can see the unified layout of the Blueprint UI:

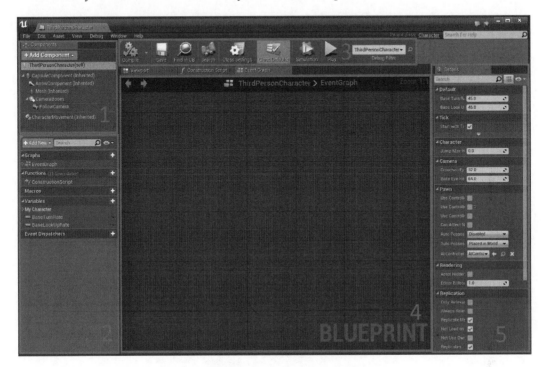

Let's take a look at these tabs:

- **Components**
- **My Blueprint**
- **Toolbar**
- **Graph editor**
- **Details panel**

Components tab

Most Blueprint classes can have different types of components. These can be light components, mesh components, UI components, and so on. In this section, we will see what they are and how we can use them in our Blueprint classes.

What are components?

Components are the bits and pieces that make up the whole Actor. Components cannot exist on their own but when added to an Actor, the Actor will then have access to all the functionalities provided by the component. For example, think about a car. The wheels, body, lights, and so on can be considered as components and the car itself as the Actor. Then in the graph, you can access the component and do the logic for your car Actor. Components are always instanced and each Actor instance will have its own unique instance of components. If this were not the case, then, if we place multiple car Actors in world and if one starts moving, all the others will also move.

Adding a component

To add a component to your Actor, click the **Add Component** button on the **Components** tab. After clicking the button it will show a list of various **Components** that you can add.

After adding a component, you will be prompted to give it a name. Components can also be directly added simply by dragging-and-dropping from **Content Browser** to the **Components** window.

To rename a component, you can select it in the **Components** tab and press *F2*.

 The drag-and-drop method only applies to **StaticMeshes**, **SkeletalMeshes**, **SoundCues**, and **ParticleSystems**.

With the component selected, you can delete it by pressing the *Delete* key. You can also right-click on the component and select **Delete** to remove it as well.

Transforming the component

Once the component is added and selected, you can use the transform tools (*W, E,* and *R*) to change the location, rotation, and scale of the component either by entering values in the **Details** panel or in the **Viewport** tab. When using moving, rotating, or scaling, you can press *Shift* to enable snapping, provided you have enabled grid snapping in the **Viewport** toolbar.

 If the Component has any child components attached to it then moving, rotating or scaling that component will propagate the transformation to all child components too.

Adding events for components

Adding events based on a component is very easy and can be done by different methods. Events created in this manner are specific to that component and need not be tested as to which component is involved:

- **Adding events from the details panel**: When you select the component you will see all the events available for that component in the **Details** panel as buttons. When you click on any of them, the editor will create the event node specific for that component in the event graph.

- **Adding events by right-clicking**: When you right-click on a component, you will see **Add Event** in the context menu. From there you can select any event you want and editor will create the event node specific to that component in the event graph.

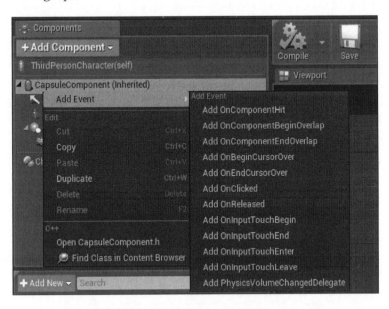

- **Adding events in the graph**: Once you select your component in the **My Blueprints** tab, you can right-click on the graph and get all the **Events** for that component.

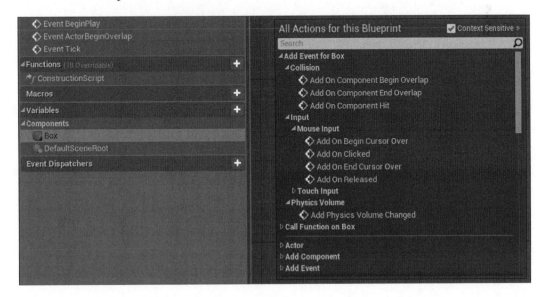

My Blueprints tab

The **My Blueprints** tab displays a list of **Graphs**, **Functions**, **Macros**, **Variables**, and so on that are contained within your Blueprint. This tab is dependent on the type of Blueprint. For example, a class Blueprint will have **EventGraph**, **ConstructionScript Graph**, **Variables**, **Functions**, **Macros**, and so on. An interface will only show the list of functions within it. A **Macro Library** will show only the macros created within it.

Creation buttons

You can create new variables, functions, macros, event graphs, and event dispatchers inside the **My Blueprints** tab by clicking the shortcut button (+).

You can also add them by clicking the **+Add New** drop-down button.

Searching in my Blueprint

The **My Blueprint** tab also provides a search area to search for your variables, functions, macros, event graphs, and event dispatchers. You can search based on name, comment, or any other data.

Categorizing in My Blueprint

It is always a good practice to organize your variables, functions, macros, event dispatchers, and so on into various categories. In the **My Blueprints** tab, you can have as many categories with sub-categories. Check the following screenshot:

Here you can see how I have organized everything into various categories and sub-categories. To set a category for your variables, functions, macros, and event dispatchers, simply select them and in the **Details** panel you can type your new category name or select from an existing category. If you need sub-categories then you need to separate your sub-category name with a vertical bar key (|). For example, if you want **Health** as a sub-category in **Attributes**, you can set it like this: **Attributes** | **Health**.

Toolbar

The toolbar provides access to common commands required while editing Blueprints. Toolbar buttons will be different depending on which mode (editing mode, play in editor mode, and so on) is active and which Blueprint type you are currently editing.

Graph editor

Graph editor is the main area of your Blueprint. This is where you add new nodes and connect them to create the network that defines the scripted behavior. More information on how to create new nodes and various nodes will be explained later on in this book.

Details panel

The **Details** panel provides access to properties of the selected **Components** or **Variables**. It contains a search field so you can search for a specific property.

Blueprint graph types

As we mentioned before, Blueprints are assets that are saved in **Content Browser** that are used to create new types of Actors or script gameplay logic, events, and so on, giving both designers and programmers the ability to quickly iterate gameplay without writing a single line of code. In order for a Blueprint to have scripted behavior, we need to define how it behaves using various nodes in graph editor. Let's take a quick look at various graphs:

- **Construction Script Graph**: Construction graph is executed the moment the Blueprint is initialized and whenever a change happens to any variables within the Blueprint. This means that whenever you place an instance of the Blueprint in the level and change its transformation or any variable, the construction graph is executed. This graph is executed once every time it is constructed and again when any of the properties or Blueprint is updated. This can be used to construct procedural elements or to set up values before the game begins.

- **Event Graph**: This is where all the gameplay logic is contained, including interactivity and dynamic responses. Using various event nodes as entry points to functions, flow controls, and variables, you can script the behavior of the Blueprint. Event graphs are only executed when you start the game.

- **Function Graph**: By default, this graph contains one single entry point with the name of the function. This node can never be deleted but you can move it around freely. Nodes in this graph are only executed when you call this function in the construction or event graph or from another Blueprint that is referencing the Blueprint that this function belongs to.

- **Macro Graph**: This is like a collapsed graph that contains your nodes. Unlike function graphs, macros can have multiple inputs or outputs.

- **Interface Graph**: Interface graphs are disabled and you cannot move, create graphs, variables, or components.

 Only class Blueprints have **Construction Script** and it stops executing when gameplay begins and is considered completed before gameplay.

Function graph

Function graphs are node graphs created inside a Blueprint and can be executed from another graph (such as **Event Graph** or **Construction Script**) or from another Blueprint. By default, function graphs contain a single execution pin that is activated when the function is called, causing the connected nodes to execute.

Creating functions

Function graphs are created through **My Blueprints** tab and you can create as many functions as you want.

Inside **My Blueprints** tab you can hover your mouse over the functions header and click on **+Function** to add a new function

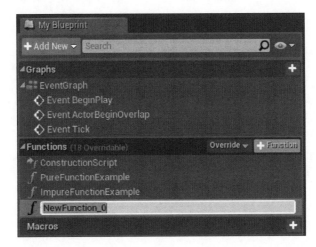

Clicking that button (the yellow highlighted button) will create a new function and prompts you to enter a new name for it.

Graph settings

When you create a new function and select it, you will get some properties of that function, which you can change in the **Details** panel. Let's take a quick look at them.

- **Description**: Appears as a tooltip when you hover your mouse over this function in another graph.

- **Category**: Keeps this function in its given category (for organizational purpose only).

- **Access Specifier**: Sometimes when you create functions, you don't want to access some of them in another Blueprint. Access specifiers let you specify what other objects can access this function.

- **Public**: This means any object can access this function from anywhere. This is the default setting.

- **Protected**: This means current Blueprint and any Blueprints derived from the current Blueprint can access this function.

- **Private**: This setting means only the current Blueprint can access this function.

- **Pure**: When enabled, this function is marked as a **Pure Function** and when disabled it is an **Impure Function**.

    ◦ **Pure Function** will not modify state or members of a class in any way and is considered a **Constant Function** that only outputs a data value and does not have an execution pin. These are connected to other **Data Pins** and are automatically executed when the data on them is required.

    ◦ **Impure Function** is free to modify any value in a class and contains an execution pin.

The following is a screenshot showing the difference between **Pure Function** and **Impure Function**:

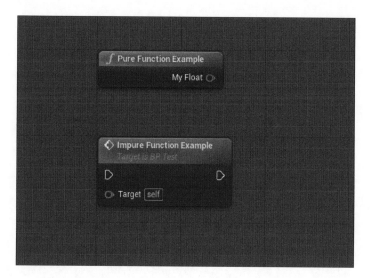

Editing functions

To define the functionality of the function you need to edit it. You can have as many inputs or outputs as you want, and can then create a node network between those inputs and outputs to define the functionality. To add input or output, you first need to select the function either in the **My Blueprint** tab or select the main pink node when you open the **Function Graph**. Then, in the **Details** panel, you will see a button labelled **New** that creates new inputs or outputs.

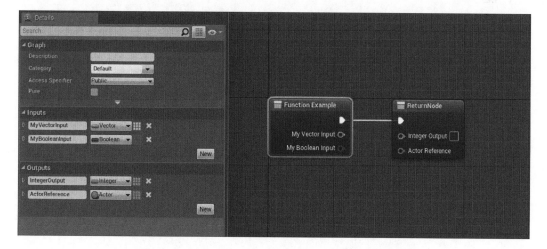

In this screenshot you can see how I added new inputs and outputs to **Function Example**.

> **ReturnNode** is optional and will only appear if you have at least one output data pin. If you remove all output pins then **ReturnNode** is automatically removed and you can still use your function.

For example, in the following screenshot I created a Blueprint function that appends a prefix to my character name so I can use this one single function to change the prefix anytime I want.

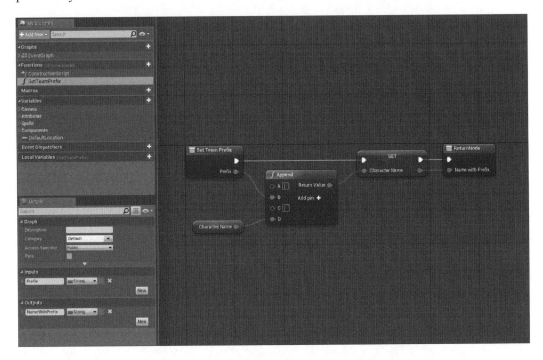

Now, back in **Event Graph**, I call this function on the **Begin Play** event so I can set the character name when the game starts.

Macro graph

Macro graphs are essentially collapsed graphs of nodes, which contain an entry point and exit point designated by tunnel nodes but cannot contain variables. Macro graphs can have any number of execution or data pins.

Macros can be created inside a **Class Blueprint** or **Level Blueprint** like functions or you can organize your **Macros** in a **Blueprint Macro Library**, which can be created in **Content Browser**.

Blueprint Macro Library can contain all your **Macros** in one place so you can use them in any other Blueprint. These can be real time-savers as they can contain most commonly used nodes and can transfer data. But changes to a macro graph are only reflected when the Blueprint containing that macro is recompiled.

To create a macro library you need to right-click in **Content Browser** and select **Blueprint Macro Library** from the Blueprints sub-category.

Once you select that option you have to select a parent class for your Macro. Most of the time we select Actor as the parent class. After the selection, you will be prompted to type a name for your Macro library and save it.

If you just created your Macro library, the editor will create a blank Macro named **NewMacro_0** and will be highlighted for you to rename.

As you did with functions, you can type a description and define a **Category** for your Macro. You also get an option to define a color for your Macro using **Instance Color**.

In the following screenshot you can see I created a Macro with multiple outputs and defined a **Description**, **Category**, and an **Instance Color** for the Macro:

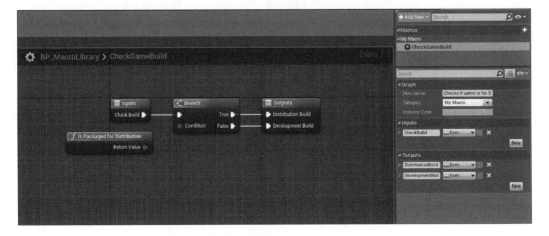

In any other Blueprint I can now get this Macro and use it. If you hover you mouse over the Macro, you can see the description you set as a **Tooltip**.

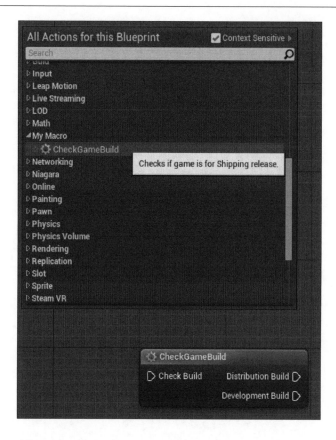

Interface graph

Interface graphs are a collection of functions without any implementation, which can be added to other Blueprints. Any Blueprint class implementing an interface will definitely contain all the functions from the interface. It is then up to the user to give functionality to the functions in that interface. Interface editor is similar to other Blueprints but you cannot add new variables, edit the graph, or add any components.

Interfaces are used to communicate between various Blueprints that share specific functionality. For example, if the player is having a **Flame Thrower** gun and in the game you have **Ice** and **Cloth**, both can take damage but one should melt and the other should burn. You can create a **Blueprint Interface** that contains a **TakeWeaponFire** function and have **Ice** and **Cloth** implement this interface. Then, in **Ice Blueprint**, you can implement the **TakeWeaponFire** function and make the ice melt and, in **Cloth Blueprint**, you can implement that same function and make the cloth burn. Now when you are firing your **Flame Thrower** you can simply call the **TakeWeaponFire** function and it calls them in those Blueprints.

To create a new interface, you need to right-click on the **Content Browser** and select **Blueprint Interface** from the Blueprints sub-category and then name it.

In the following example I named it **BP_TestInterface**:

If you just created your interface the editor will create a blank function named **NewFunction_0**, which will be highlighted for you to rename. If you implement this interface on any Blueprint then it will have this function.

In this example, I created a function called **MyInterfaceFunction**. We will use this to simply print out the Actor name that implements this interface.

To create functionality for this function, we first need to implement this interface in a Blueprint. So open your Blueprint where you want this to be implemented and select **Class Settings** in the **Toolbar**.

Now the **Details** panel will show the settings for this Blueprint and, under the **Interfaces** section, you can add your interface.

Once you add that interface, the **My Blueprints** tab will update to show you the interface functions. Now all you have to do is double-click on the function to open the graph and add functionality.

The reason why **MyInterfaceFunction** appears in the **My Blueprints** tab is because that function contains an output value. If you have an interface function without an output then it won't appear in the **My Blueprints** tab. Instead it appears under **Events** when right-clicking in your Blueprint. For example, in that same interface I created another function without output data.

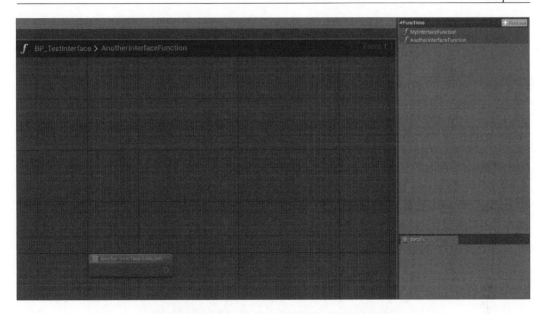

This **AnotherInterfaceFunction** will not appear in the **My Blueprints** tab because it has no output. So, to implement this function in your Blueprint, you have to add this as an event.

Blueprint node references

The behavior of a Blueprint object is defined using various nodes. Nodes can be **Events**, **Function Calls**, **Flow Control**, **Variables**, and so on that are used in the graph. Even though each type of node has a unique function, the way they are created and used is common.

Nodes are added to the graph by right-clicking inside the graph panel and selecting the node from the **Context Menu**. If a component inside Blueprint is selected, events and functions supported by that component are also listed.

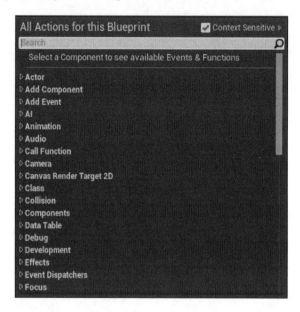

After a node is added you can select it and move it around using the left mouse button. You can use *Ctrl* to add or remove from the current selection of nodes. Clicking and dragging inside the graph creates a **Marquee Selection** that adds to the current selection.

Nodes can have multiple inputs and outputs and are of two types: **Execution Pins** and **Data Pins**.

Execution pins start the flow of execution and when the execution is completed it activates an output execution pin to continue the flow. Execution pins are drawn as outlines when not wired and solid white when connected.

Data pins are nodes that transfer (such as taking and outputting) data from one node to the other. These nodes are type specific. That means they can be connected to variables of the same type. Some data pins are automatically converted if you connect them to another data pin that is not of the same type. For example, if you connect a `float` variable to `string`, the Blueprint editor will automatically insert a `float` to a `string` conversion node. Like execution pins, they are drawn as an outline when not connected, and a solid color when connected.

Node colors

Nodes in Blueprint have different colors that show what kind of node it is.

A red-colored node means it's an event node and this is where execution starts.

A blue-colored node means it can either be a function or an event being called. These nodes can have multiple inputs or outputs. The icon on top of the function will be changed based on whether it's a function or event.

A purple-colored node can neither be created nor destroyed. You can see this node in **Construction Script** and **Functions**.

A grey node can be a **Macro**, **Flow Control**, or **Collapsed** node.

A green-colored node usually means a Pure function used to get a value.

A cyan-colored node means it's a cast node. This node converts the given object to another.

Variables

Variables are properties that hold a value or an object reference. They can be accessed inside the Blueprint editor or from another Blueprint. They can be created to include data types (`float`, `integer`, `Boolean`, and so on) or reference types or classes. Each variable can also be an array. All types are color coded for easy identification.

Math expression

Math expression nodes are essentially collapsed nodes that you can double-click to open the sub graph to see the functionality. Whenever you rename the node, the new expression is parsed and a new graph is generated. To rename the node, simply select it and press *F2*.

To create a **Math Expression** node, right-click on the graph editor and select **Add Math Expression** node. You will then be prompted to type your **Math Expression**.

For example, let's type this expression: *(vector(x, y, z)) + ((a + 1) * (b + 1))* and press *Enter*.

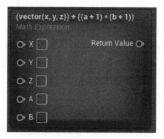

You will now see that the **Math Expression** node has automatically parsed your expression and generated proper variables and a graph from your expression.

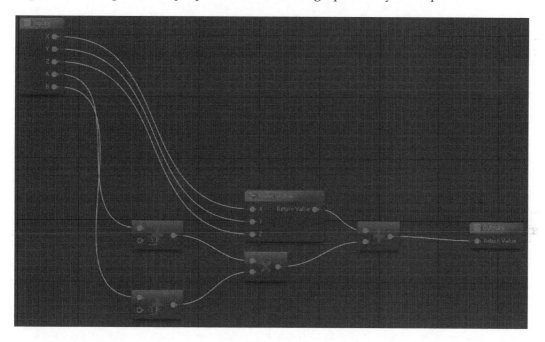

The following operators are supported and can be combined with logical and comparison operators to create complex expressions:

- **Multiplicative**: *, /, % (modulo)
- **Additive**: +, -
- **Relational**: <, >, <=, >=
- **Equality**: == (equal), != (not equal)
- **Logical**: | | (or), && (and), ^ (power)

Creating our first Blueprint class

Now that we have an idea of what Blueprint is and what it does, let's create a simple Blueprint actor that spins on its own and destroys itself after a few seconds with a particle effect and sound. After creating our Blueprint, we will drag and drop this into the world and we will also use the **Level Blueprint** to dynamically spawn this Blueprint while running the game.

Creating a new Blueprint

To create this Blueprint, first right-click inside **Content Browser** and select **Blueprint Class**. Once you click that you will be prompted to select a parent class for the Blueprint. You need to specify a parent class for your Blueprint as it will inherit all properties from that parent class.

Even though you can choose all existing classes (even other Blueprint classes), let's take a look at the most common parent classes:

- **Actor**: An Actor-based Blueprint can be placed or spawned in the level
- **Pawn**: **Pawn** is what you can call an agent which you can possess and receives inputs from the controller
- **Character**: This is an extended version of **Pawn** with the ability to walk, run, jump, crouch, and more
- **Player Controller**: This is used to control the **Character** or **Pawn**
- **Game Mode**: This defines the game being played
- **Actor Component**: This is a reusable component that can be added to any actor
- **Scene Component**: This is a component with scene transform and can be attached to other scene components

In this example, we will use the **Actor** class as our parent because we want to place it in the level and spawn at runtime. So choose **Actor** class and Unreal will create and place your new Blueprint in **Content Browser**. Double-click on your newly created Blueprint and this will open the Blueprint editor. By default, it should open the **Viewport** tab but if it doesn't then simply select the **Viewport** tab. This is where you can see and manipulate all of your components.

Now we need a component that will spin when this Blueprint is spawned. On the **Components** tab, click **Add Component** and select **Static Mesh** component. After you add the component, rename it to **Mesh Component** (you can choose whatever name you want but, for this example, let's choose that name) and note how the **Details** panel has been populated with **Static Mesh** properties.

In the **Details** panel, you can find the section that corresponds to your component type where you can assign the asset to use.

But, in this example, instead of directly assigning a mesh in the **Components** tab, we create a **Static Mesh** variable and use that to assign the mesh in the graph. This way, we can change the mesh without opening the Blueprint editor.

In the **My Blueprints** tab, create a new variable and set the type to **Static Mesh** (make sure to select **reference**).

 In versions before Unreal Engine 4.9, you can search for **Static Mesh** and simply select the reference. There was no additional options to select before 4.9.

After that, rename that variable to **My Mesh**. Since this variable is used to assign the asset to use with our **Static Mesh** component, let's expose this variable so that we can change it in the **Details** panel after placing it in world. To expose this variable, select it and enable **Editable** in the **Details** panel inside the Blueprint editor. After making it editable, compile the Blueprint (shortcut key: *F7*) and you will be able to assign a default mesh for the **My Mesh** variable. For this example, let's add a simple cube **Static Mesh**.

Now that our variable is set, we can assign it to our **Static Mesh** component. Since we know that **Construction Graph** is executed every time this Blueprint is initialized and whenever a variable or property is changed, that is where we are going to assign the mesh for our **Static Mesh** component. So, open the **Construction Graph** and:

- Right-click on the graph editor and search for the **Get Mesh** component.
- Select **Get Mesh** component from the context menu.
- Click and drag from the output pin and release it. You will now see a new context menu and, in that resulting menu, search for **Set Static Mesh** and select it.
- Right-click again on graph editor and search for **Get My Mesh**.
- Select **Get My Mesh** and connect the output pin to the input (**New Mesh**) of the **Set Static Mesh** Blueprint node.
- And, finally, connect the execution pin of **Construction Script** to **Set Static Mesh Blueprint** node and press **Compile** (shortcut key: *F7*).

If you check the **Viewport** tab after compiling, you will see your new mesh there. From this point, feel free to drag this Blueprint to the world and in the **Details** panel you can change **My Mesh** to any other **Static Mesh**.

[Press *Ctrl+E* to open the associated editor of the object you have selected in world.]

Spinning static mesh

In Blueprint editor, there are a couple of ways to rotate a mesh and in this section we will look into the simplest way, which is using a **Rotate Movement** component.

Open the Blueprint if you have closed it and add a new component called **Rotating Movement**. This component will make this Actor continuously rotate at a given rotation rate optionally around a specified point. This component has three main parameters that can be changed in the Blueprint graph. They are:

- **Rotation Rate**: The speed at which this will update the **Roll/Pitch/Yaw** axis.
- **Pivot Translation**: The pivot point at which we rotate. If set to zero then we rotate around the object's origin.
- **Rotation in Local Space**: Whether rotation is applied in local space or world space.

You can create two new variables (**Rotator** and **Vector** variables) and make them editable so you can change it in the **Details** panel in world. The final graph should look like this:

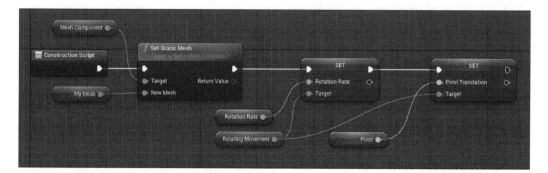

Destroying our Blueprint Actor after some seconds

Once we place or spawn this Actor in world we will destroy this actor with a particle effect and sound. To do that:

- Create a new variable (`float`) and name it **DestroyAfter**. Let's give it a default value of five seconds.

- Go to **Event Graph** and add a new event called **Event BeginPlay**. This node is immediately executed when the game starts or when the actor is spawned in the game.

- Right-click on the graph editor and search for **Delay** and add it. Connect **Event BeginPlay** to the **Delay** node. This node is used to call an action after a number of specified seconds.

- The **Delay** node takes a `float` value, which is used for the duration. After the duration runs out, execution is continued to the next action. We will connect our **DestroyAfter** variable to the duration of **Delay**.

- Right-click on the graph and search for **Spawn Emitter At Location**. This node will spawn the given particle effect at the specified location and rotation. Connect **Delay** to this node and set a particle effect by assigning it in the **Emitter Template**. To set the location, right-click on the graph and search for **GetActorLocation** and connect it to **Location pin**.

- Right-click on the graph and search for **Spawn Sound At Location**. This node will spawn and play a sound at the given location. Connect **Spawn Emitter** node to this one.

- And, finally, to destroy this actor, right-click on the graph editor and search for **DestroyActor** and connect it to **Spawn Sound** node.

The final graph should look like this:

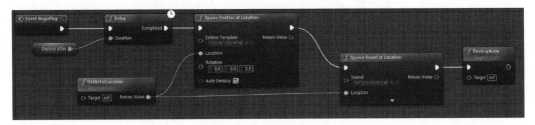

Now, when you place this actor in world and start the game you will see it spin and, after five seconds (or the value you used in **Destroy After**), this actor will be destroyed after spawning the particle effect and sound.

Spawning our Blueprint class in Level Blueprint

We will now see how we can spawn this Blueprint Actor in world while the game is running, instead of directly placing when editing.

Before we continue we will make a change to the **DestroyAfter** variable in our spinning Blueprint Actor. Open our spinning actor's Blueprint editor and, in **Variables**, select the **DestroyAfter** variable and, in the **Details** panel, enable the **Expose On Spawn** setting.

This setting means this variable will be exposed in the **Spawn Actor** node.

Open your level and, on the toolbar, click the Blueprints button and select **Open Level** Blueprint. In **Level Blueprint** perform the following steps:

- Right-click on the graph and search for **Event BeginPlay** and add it.
- Right-click on the graph and search for **Spawn Actor** from **Class** and add it. This node will spawn the given actor class at the specified location, rotation and scale.
- In the class pin set the class to our **Rotating Blueprint** Actor. Note how the **Destroy After** variable is now exposed to **Spawn** node. You can now adjust that value from that **Spawn** node.
- Drag from the **Spawn Transform** node and release the left mouse button. From the resulting context menu, select **Make Transform**. The transform node contains 3D transformation including translation, rotation, and scale. For this example, let's set the **Location** to **0,0,300** so that is this Actor will be spawned 300 units above the ground.

The resulting graph should look like this:

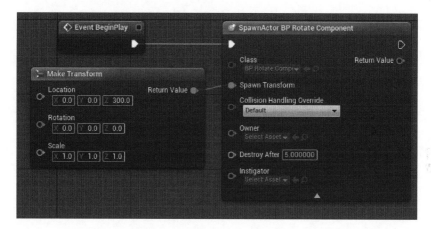

If you play (*Alt+P*) or simulate (*Alt+S*) you will see this rotating Actor spawn **300** units above the ground and spinning.

Summary

In this chapter, we have learned what components are and how we can use them to define a Blueprint Actor. We also learned about Blueprint nodes and how you can create them. From what you have learned in this chapter, you can take it even further by:

- Spawning this actor when overlapping a trigger volume placed in the level
- Playing a particle and sound effect when spawning this Blueprint
- Applying damage to a player if the player is in a certain radius

In the next chapter, we will use Matinee to create a cut scene.

7
Matinee

Matinee provides the ability to keyframe various properties of actors over time, either dynamically in gameplay or in cinematic game sequences. The system is based on specialized tracks in which you can place keyframes on certain properties of an actor. The **user interface (UI)** of Matinee is similar to other nonlinear video editing software, which makes it easier and familiar for video editors.

In this chapter, we will create a Matinee sequence and learn how we can play it through **Level Blueprint**. So to get started, let's start Unreal Engine 4 and create a new project based on **Third Person Template**.

Creating a new Matinee

To open the Matinee UI, we first need to create the Matinee asset. You can create a Matinee asset by clicking on the **Matinee** button and selecting **Add Matinee** in the level editor toolbar. When you click on it, you might get a warning saying that Undo/Redo data will be reset. This is because, while you are in the Matinee mode, some changes are translated into keyframes and editor needs to clear the undo stack. Click on **Continue** and a new Matinee Actor will be placed in the level and the Matinee editor will open. Let's take a closer look at the Matinee window:

Creating new Matinee Actor

This is the Matinee Actor icon:

Matinee Actor placed in world

After creating a new Matinee Actor, it will automatically open the **Matinee** Window. If it doesn't, then select the **Matinee Actor** in world and click on **Open Matinee** in the **Details** panel.

Matinee window

Let's take a quick look at the Matinee window:

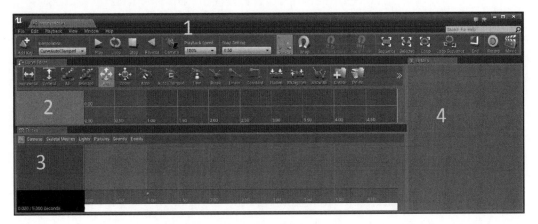

The Matinee window consists of:

- **Toolbar**: This contains all the common buttons for Matinee editor, such as playing the Matinee, stopping it, and so on. Let's take a closer look at the toolbar buttons:
    - ○ **Add key**: This adds a new keyframe at the current selected track.
    - ○ **Interpolation**: This sets the default interpolation mode when adding new keys.
    - ○ **Play**: This plays a preview from the current position in the track view at normal speed to the end of the sequence.
    - ○ **Loop**: This loops the preview in the loop section.
    - ○ **Stop**: This stops the preview playback. Clicking twice will rewind the sequence and place the time bar at the beginning of Matinee.
    - ○ **Reverse**: This reverses the preview playback.
    - ○ **Camera**: This creates a new camera Actor in world.
    - ○ **Playback Speed**: This adjusts the playback speed.
    - ○ **Snap Setting**: This sets the timeline scale for snapping.
    - ○ **Curves**: This toggles curve editor.

- ○ **Snap**: This toggles snapping of time cursor and keys.

- ○ **Time to frames**: This snaps the timeline cursor to the setting selected in the **Snap Setting** dropdown. It is only enabled if **Snap Setting** is using frames per second.

- ○ **Fixed Time**: This locks playback of Matinee to the frame rate specified in **Snap Setting**. It is only enabled if **Snap Setting** is using frames per second.

- ○ **Sequence**: This fits the timeline view to the entire sequence.

- ○ **Selected**: This fits the timeline view to the selected keys.

- ○ **Loop**: This fits the timeline view to the loop section.

- ○ **Loop sequence**: This automatically sets the start and end of the loop section to the entire sequence.

- ○ **End**: This moves to the end of the track.

- ○ **Record**: Opens the **Matinee Recorder** window.

- ○ **Movie**: This allows you to export the Matinee as a movie or image sequences.

Since Matinee is similar to other nonlinear video editors, you can use the following common shortcut keys:

> *J* to play the sequence backward
>
> *K* to stop/pause
>
> *L* to play the sequence forward
>
> Plus (+) to zoom in to the time line
>
> Minus (-) to zoom out of the time line

- **Curve editor**: This allows you to visualize and edit the animation curves used by tracks in the Matinee sequence. This allows for fine control over properties that change over time. Certain tracks with animation curves can be edited in curve Editor by toggling the **Curve** button. Clicking on it will send the curve information to curve editor where the curve will be visible to the user.

- **Tracks** This is the heart of the Matinee window. This is where you set all your keyframes for your tracks and organize them into tabs, groups, and folders. By default, when you create a Matinee, the length is set to 5 seconds.

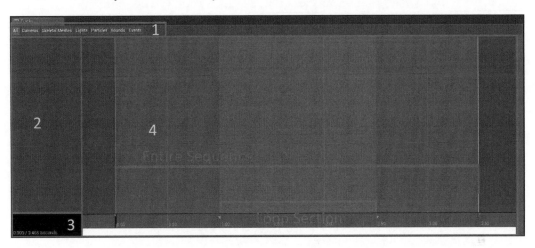

- ○ **Tabs**: These are used for organization purposes. You can put your tracks into various tabs. For example, you can put all your lights in your Matinee to the **Lights** tab, camera to the **Camera** tab, and so on. The **All** tab will show all tracks in your sequence.

- ○ **Track List**: This is where you create tracks that can create keyframes in the timeline and organize them into different groups. You can also create new folders and organize all groups into separate folders.

- ○ **Timeline Info**: This shows information about the timeline including the current time, where the cursor is, and the total length of the sequence.

- ○ **Timeline**: This shows all the tracks within the sequence and this is where we manipulate objects, animate cameras, and so on using keyframes. The green area shows the loop section (in between the green markers). At the bottom of track view, you can see a small black bar, which is called the **Time Bar**. If you click on and hold it, you can scrub the timeline forward or backward, which allows you to quickly preview the animation. To adjust the length of the sequence, you move the far right red marker to the length you want this Matinee to be.

Manipulating an object

Matinee can be used to create cut scenes where you move the camera and manipulate objects or it can be used for simple gameplay elements such as opening doors and moving lifts. In this example, we will see how we can move a simple cube from one location to another location.

From **Engine Content**, we will drag and drop the **Cube** mesh into our world. This is located in the `Engine Content\BasicShapes` folder.

To get **Engine Content**, you need to enable it in **Content Browser**.

1. At the bottom right corner of **Content Browser**, you can see **View Options**.
2. Click on it and then enable **Show Engine Content**.

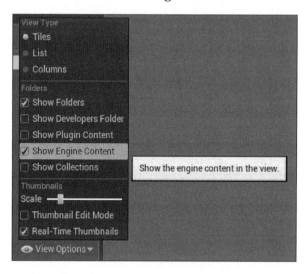

After placing our **Cube** in world, let's open the **Matinee** editor window. Make sure the **Cube** is selected in world and right-click in the track list area and select **Add New Empty Group**. You will now be prompted to type a name for your group. Let's call it **Cube_Movement**.

Note that if you see a notification at the bottom-right corner of your screen saying **Cube Mobility** has been changed to **Movable**, don't panic. Actors that are being manipulated in Matinee must set the **Mobility** to **Movable**.

If you click on this group in Matinee now, you can see the **Cube** in world will be automatically selected for you. This is because, when we created the group, we had the **Cube** selected in world and whatever object you have selected in world will automatically be hooked to the group you create.

To move the cube in world, we need to add a **Movement Track** to our **Cube_ Movement** group. To create this track:

1. Right-click on our **Empty Group (Cube_Movement)**.
2. Select **Add New Movement Track**.

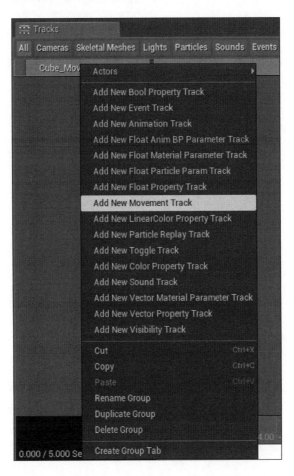

This will add a new movement track to our **Empty Group** and will set the current position of our cube as the first keyframe.

The small triangle in the beginning of the timeline is the keyframe

Now, we want the cube to move to the right by some distance and, by the end of this sequence, it should come back to its default position. So let's scrub the time bar to the middle of the sequence (since the default length is 5 seconds long, we will move the time bar to **2.5**) and go back to **Viewport** editor. There, we select and move the cube by some distance to the right side (*Y* axis) and press *Enter*. Note that now Matinee has created a new keyframe for you at the time slot **2.5** and you will see a dotted yellow line that represents the movement path of the cube.

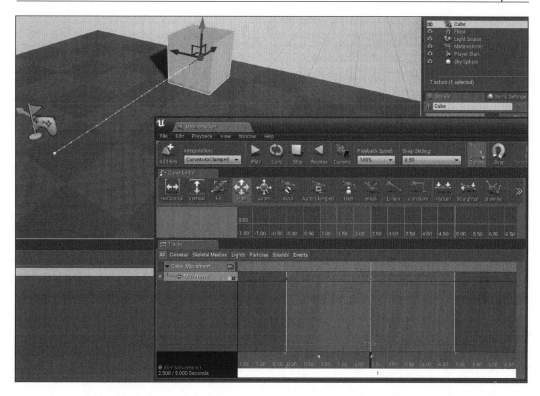

To set the keyframe at the exact time (for example, precisely at **2.5**) you can left-click on the key frame to select it and then right-click and select **Set Time**. You will now be prompted to enter the new time to set the keyframe. Here, you can type and set **2.5**.

If you scrub the time bar now, you will see the cube move from its original position to the new position that we keyframed at time **2.5**. Now, to get the cube back to its original position at the end of the sequence, we can simply copy paste the first keyframe to the end of the sequence. To do so, click on the first keyframe and press *Ctrl+C* to copy it. Then, scrub the time bar to the end of the sequence and press *Ctrl+V* to paste it. The finished Matinee should look like this:

If you hit **Play** in the toolbar now, you will see the cube move from its original location to the new location and then, by the end of sequence, it will go back to its original location.

Now that our Matinee is ready, we will see how to play the Matinee in game. What we are going to do is place a trigger box in level and, when our player overlaps it, Matinee will play. When our player steps out of the trigger box, Matinee will stop.

To place a trigger box in world, you need to drag it and drop it into the viewport from the **Modes** tab (which is under **Place** in the **Volume** category). If you don't have the **Modes** tab, then:

1. Press *Shift+1* to open it (make sure your viewport is in focus).
2. In the **Modes** tab, go to the **Place** mode (*Shift+1*).
3. Select the **Volumes** tab.
4. Drag and drop the **Trigger Volume** box.

Once the trigger box is placed in world (feel free to adjust the size of the trigger box), right-click on it and navigate to **Add Event | OnActorBeginOverlap**.

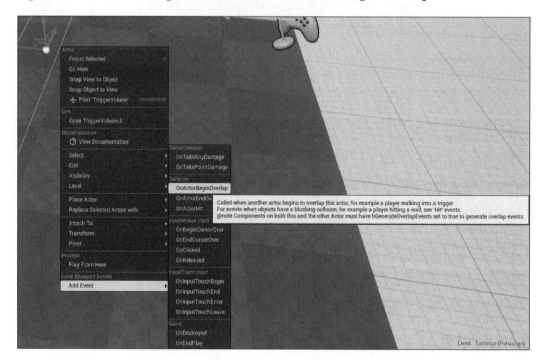

This will add a new **Overlap Event** for our **Trigger Volume** in **Level Blueprint**. Since we need to stop the Matinee after exiting the trigger, we will right-click again on the **Trigger Volume** and navigate to **Add Event | OnActorEndOverlap**. We now have two events (**Begin Overlap** and **End Overlap**) in our **Level Blueprint**.

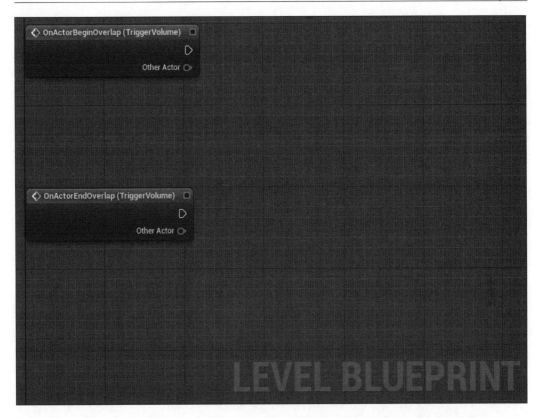

As you can see, both overlap events give us the actor that is currently overlapping this **Trigger Volume**. We will use this information to play the Matinee only when a character is overlapping. To do so, we will have to follow this process:

1. Click and drag from the other Actor pin in the **OnActorBeginOverlap** event. From the resulting context window, type **Cast to Character** and select it.

2. Connect the execution pin of **OnActorBeginOverlap** to the **Cast** node we just created.

3. To play the Matinee, we first need to create a reference of it in **Level Blueprint**. To do so, select the Matinee icon in world and right-click inside the **Level Blueprint**. From the resulting context window, select **Create a reference to Matinee Actor**. This will add a new node, which is referred to the Matinee Actor in world. From this node, drag a new wire and type **Play** and select it.

4. Connect the output (unnamed) execution pin of the **Character** node to the **Play** node of Matinee.

5. To stop the Matinee when exiting the trigger, you can do the same setup as previously, but instead of the play node, use the **Stop** node.

The final graph should look like this:

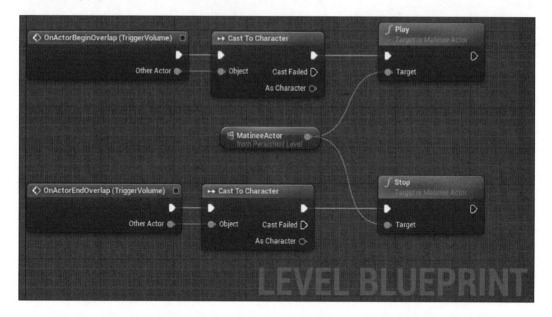

Now, when you play the game and overlap the trigger, our Matinee will play.

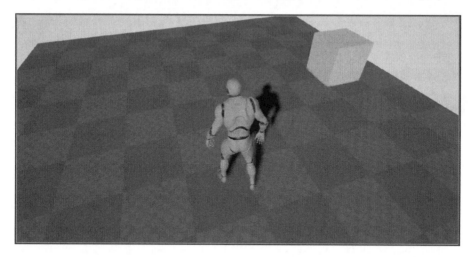

Cutscene camera

Since you have learned how to create a Matinee and move an object, it is time to learn how to create a simple cut-scene. In this section, we will create a camera that focuses on the cube when Matinee is triggered.

To create a camera, let's first position the viewport camera at the right location. In your editor **Viewport**, navigate to the place where you want the Matinee camera to be. In the following screenshot, you can take a look at where I placed the camera:

After navigating to your desired location, open the **Matinee** window. On the toolbar, click on the **Camera** button (this will prompt you to enter a new group name) to create a camera at your current **Viewport** camera location.

This will also create a new **Camera** group with two tracks. They are **Field of View (FOV)** and **Movement**. Since we don't use the FOV track, you can right-click on it and select **Delete Track**, or simply press *Delete* to remove it from the track list.

With the **Movement Track** of the camera selected, scrub the time bar to the end of the sequence. Then in the editor **Viewport**, select the camera created by Matinee and move it to a new location. In this example, I moved the camera to the right side and rotated it by 30 degrees. In the following screenshots, you can see the initial location of the camera and the new location at the end of the sequence.

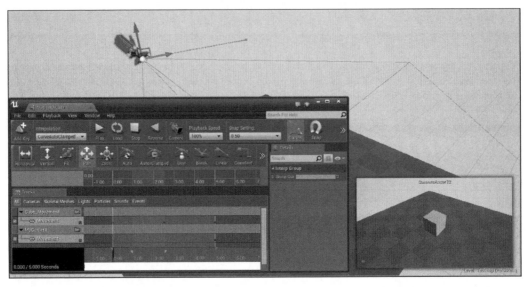

This is the new location of the camera:

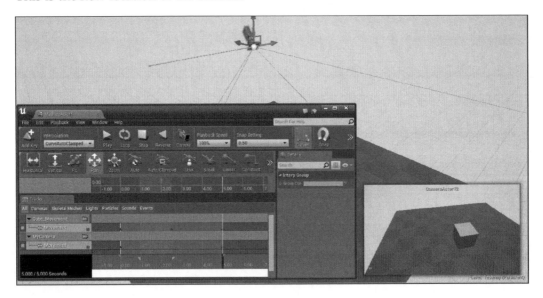

If you play now and trigger the Matinee from the **Trigger Volume** we placed earlier, you will see the cube moving as usual but you will not see it from the camera perspective. To see it through the camera we placed now, you need to add a **Director Track** to your Matinee. Let's take a look at what a **Director Group** is.

Director group

Director group serves the main function of controlling the visual and audio of your Matinee. The important function of this group is to control which camera group is chosen to be seen in the sequence. We use this group to cut between one camera and the next when we have multiple cameras in Matinee.

To create a new **Director Group**, right-click on the track list and select **Add New Director Group**. A new separate group will be opened on top of all other groups.

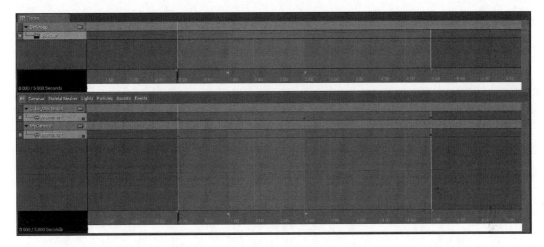

Since we only have one camera in this group, we will add that one to our director track. Select the director track and press *Enter*. A new pop up will ask you which track to choose, so select **MyCamera** group (this is the group we created using the **Camera** button in Matinee toolbar). The name **MyCamera** was something I chose. A new keyframe will be added to the director track that says **MyCamera [Shot0010]**. This means that whenever this Matinee is played, you will see through the **MyCamera** group. Later, if you add more cameras, you can switch between cameras in **Director Group**.

The end result should look like this:

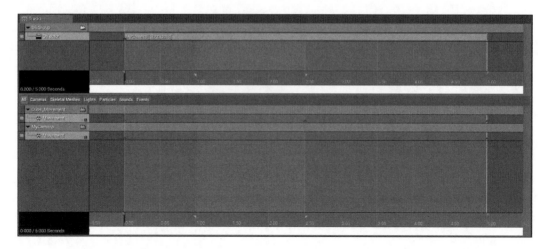

Now, if you play the Matinee in the game, you will see it through the new **Camera** view.

Sometimes, when cutscenes are played, it's better to disable **Player** movement (so that when the cutscene is active all player inputs, such as moving around, will be disabled) and HUD and all that. To do these, select the Matinee Actor in world and then in the **Details** panel, you can set the necessary options.

Summary

Matinee is a very powerful tool to create in game cinematics. With multiple cameras and other visual/audio effects, you can create good-looking and professional cinematics. Since you learned how to manipulate objects and cameras in this chapter, you should now try to create an elevator movement with a camera that acts as a CCTV.

8
Unreal Motion Graphics

Unreal Motion Graphics (UMG) is a User Interface (UI) authoring tool that is used to create in game **Heads up Display (HUDs)**, Main Menu, and other UI elements. They are created using a special blueprint called **Widget Blueprint**, which contains various predefined widgets that you can use to construct your interface. Let's take a look at UMG now.

In this chapter, you will learn how to create UMG Widgets and assign one to our character to display his health. You will also learn how to create floating health bars.

Setting up a project

To get started, start Unreal Engine 4 and create a new project based on Third Person Template.

Since we are going to have a HUD with a health bar, let's add a new health variable to our Third Person Character Blueprint. Open up the **ThirdPersonCharacter** Blueprint in the `ThirdPersonBP/Blueprints` folder:

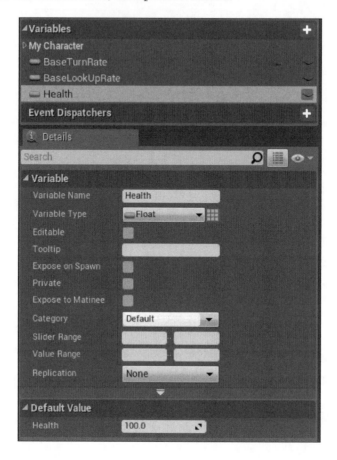

Inside our character Blueprint, create a new variable called **Health** and follow these steps:

- Set the variable type to `float` and give it a default value of 100. The next step is to create a **Pure** function that shows the percentage of the total health of the player.

- Inside your Character Blueprint, create a new function (for example, **GetHealthPercentage**) and open it.

- In the function graph, get your health variable and divide it by the default value of health. By doing so, we will get the percentage of our player health. To get the default value of any variable in your class, just right-click in graph and search for **Get Class Defaults**. This node will return all the default values of the variables you created.

- Now, create a new output for this function (float type) and connect the result (divide node) to this output. This function will now return the percentage of your player health. For example, if your player's health is 42, then dividing it by 100 (default health value) will return 0.42. We can use this information for our progress bar in HUD as well as the floating health bar.

The resulting Blueprint function should look like this:

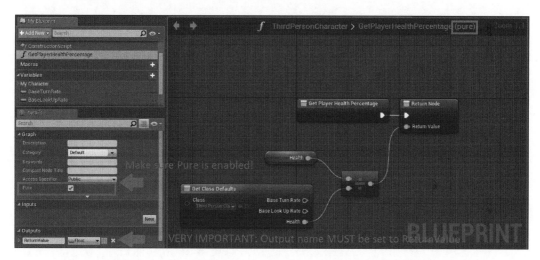

 Note that it is very important to set the output name to **ReturnValue**.

We will now create a UMG Widget and make use of this function to display the player's health.

Creating the HUD Widget

To create a new Widget Blueprint:

- Right-click on Content Browser
- Select **Widget Blueprint** under the **User Interface** section:

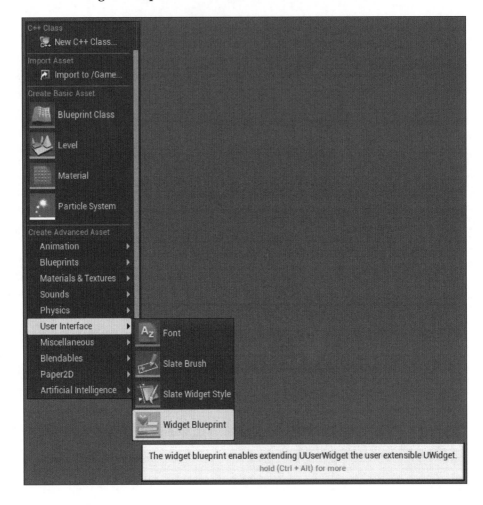

Once you select that, a new **Widget Blueprint** will be placed in Content Browser and it prompts you to enter a new name. For this example, I named it MyUMG_HUD.

Double-click on MyUMG_HUD to open it:

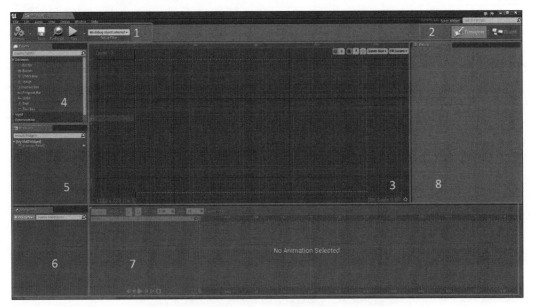

Widget Blueprint User Interface

This is Widget Blueprint. This is where you create the UI for your game. Let's take a closer look at Widget Blueprint UI:

- **Toolbar**: This is the common toolbar that lets you **Compile**, **Save**, **Play**, and **Debug** your graph.

- **Editor Mode**: This lets you switch between the **Designer** mode and the **Graph** mode.

- **Visual Designer**: This is the main area where you drag and drop all the widgets to create your UI as it appears in the game.

- **Palette**: This is the list of widgets that you can drag and drop into **Visual Designer**. This will also list any custom widgets you have created.

- **Hierarchy**: This displays the structure of this widget. You can drag and drop widgets in this too.

- **Animation List**: This lets you create new **Animation Tracks**, which you can use to animate various properties of widgets.

- **Animation Track Editor**: After creating a new Animation, you can select that Animation and create key frames here.

Since we will be using this as our player HUD, let's create a progress bar that shows the player's health.

Creating the health bar

From the **Palette** window, drag and drop the **Progress Bar** widget on to the **Visual Designer**. Once placed on the **Visual Designer**, you can resize it to any size you want. You can also place it anywhere, but, for this example, I decided to keep it at the bottom-left corner of the screen.

When you select the **Progress Bar** widget, you will see all the properties that you can edit in **Details Panel** including the name of your **Progress Bar**. For this example, I have changed the name of our progress bar to HealthBar. The **Progress Bar** widget offers a variety of settings that you can change including the look and feel.

The following screenshot is from the health bar that I have just placed:

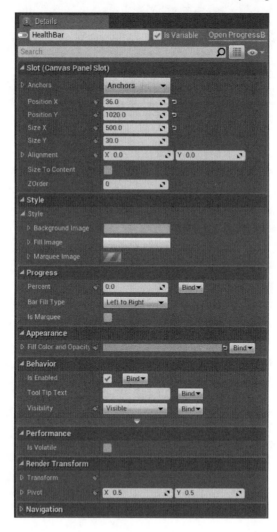

Let's take a quick look at some of the common settings that you will change:

Anchors: These define the location of the widget and maintain it for varying screen sizes. By default, there are 16 anchor positions and, typically, one of these is sufficient for most needs. But there are times where you have to adjust the Anchor position manually. For example, if your game has an inventory system where the player can dynamically resize the contents, then you need to tweak the Anchor position manually. For this example, we will set the Anchor position to the lower-left corner of the screen.

- **Position X**: This positions the widget on the *X Axis*. (horizontal).
- **Position Y**: This positions the widget on the *Y Axis*. (vertical).
- **Size X**: This scales the widget on the *X Axis*.
- **Size Y**: This scales the widget on the *Y Axis*.
- **Alignment**: This is the pivot point of the widget. Setting both **X** and **Y** to 0.0 will set the pivot point to the upper left corner and setting both to 1.0 will set the pivot point to the lower-right corner. You can use the alignment option with Anchors to precisely set a widget to the center of the screen. For example, you can set alignment (both **X** and **Y**) to 0.5 and Anchors to the center and set both position **X** and **Y** to 0.0. This will bring your widget exactly to the center of the screen. This can be used for setting a crosshair.
- **Size to Content**: If enabled, this widget will ignore **Size X** and **Size Y** values and, instead, scale according to the Widget content. For example, if your widget is a **Text Block**, then it will scale automatically according to the size of the given text.
- **ZOrder**: This defines the render priority for this widget. Higher priority widgets are rendered last, which makes them appear on top of other widgets.
- **Style**: This defines the look and feel of this widget. Note that each widget has its own unique style settings (you can either use a **Texture** or **Material** to use as an image for your widget). If it's a progress bar widget, then style category will let you change the progress bar fill image, background image, and marquee image. If it was a button, then you can change the image of the button based on the button state. For example, **Normal** state, **Hover** state, **Pressed** state, and so on.
- **Percent**: This fills the progress bar with the given value. It ranges from 0-1. In this example, we will use the **Health Percentage** of our character to drive this value.

- **Bar Fill Type**: This defines how the progress bar fills. For example, from left to right, right to left, from the center, and more.

- **Is Marquee**: This enables the marquee animation progress bar. This means that the progress bar will show activity but does not indicate when it will stop.

- **Fill Color and Opacity**: This defines the color and opacity for the fill image of the progress bar.

Now that we know the **Progress Bar** settings, let's continue and assign the Health Percentage of our character to the health bar we created. To do that, first let's switch our **Editor** mode to **Graph** mode by clicking on the **Graph** button on the top-left corner of Widget Blueprint. Once you click, you will see the Blueprint graph editor for this widget.

On the left side of the widget Blueprint, you will see the **My Blueprint** tab. As you have learned previously in the chapter on Blueprints, this is where you create your variables. So let's create a new variable (I named it `MyCharacter`) and set the type for our **Third Person Character**. See the following screenshot for reference:

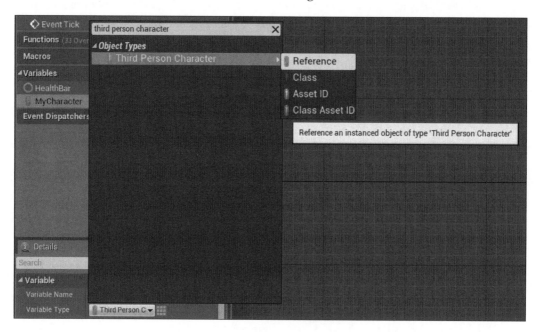

Once you create that, go back to the **Designer** mode and select your **Progress Bar**. In the **Details Panel**, you can see a **Bind** option near the **Percent** value. When you click on it, you will see a new dropdown menu that shows our newly created `MyCharacter` variable. Move your mouse over it and you will see the **GetPlayerHealthPercentage** function, which we created previously:

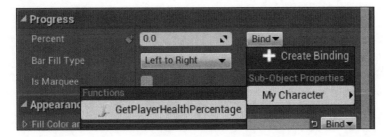

Once you click on that, it will set the Health Percentage value from our character to the progress bar.

 If you don't see your character variable in the **Bind** dropdown, make sure you compiled the **Widget Blueprint**.

Assigning our HUD to Character

Now that we have finished setting up the HUD, it is time we assign it to the character. Let's close **Widget Blueprint** for now and open **ThirdPersonCharacter Blueprint**.

Inside our **Character Blueprint**, open the **Event Graph** and:

- Right-click and, from the resulting context menu, search for **Event BeginPlay** and select it.

- Drag a wire from the execution pin of **Event BeginPlay** and release the mouse button. From the context menu, search for **Create Widget** and select it.

- In the **Create Widget** node, select **MyUMG_HUD** in the class pin.

- From the **Return Value** of the **Create Widget** node, drag a new wire and release the mouse button. From the context menu, search for **Set My Character** and select it.

- Right-click on the graph editor and search for `self` and select **Get a reference to self**. Connect this node to the **My Character** pin.

- Again, drag a wire from the **Return Value** of the **Create Widget** node and search for **Add to Viewport**.

- Connect the output execution pin of the **Set My Character** node to the input execution pin of **Add to Viewport**.

The resulting graph should look like this:

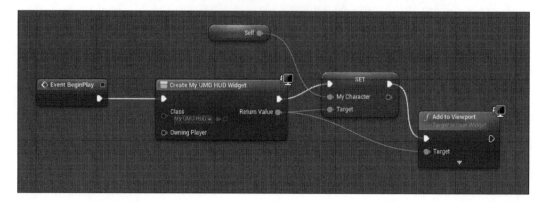

Now, if you play the game, you will see the health bar filled completely:

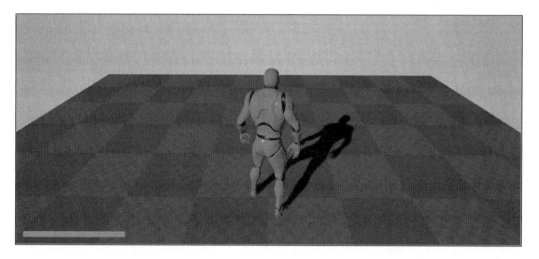

 If your health bar is still empty, make sure you set the output name of **GetHealthPercentage** to **ReturnValue**.

To test it, we can create a new function called **DecrementHealth** and create a graph like this:

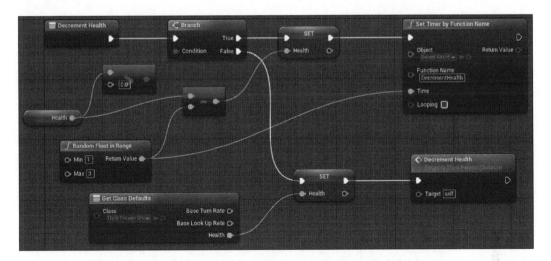

After that, drag and drop this function from your **My Blueprints** tab and connect it after the **Add to Viewport** node. Now, if you start playing, you will see the player health going down randomly.

Creating floating health bars

In this section, you will learn how to create a floating health bar above the character's head. Let's go back to **Content Browser** and create a new **Widget Blueprint** (for this example, I'll name it **MyFloatingHealthbar**) and open it.

In the **Designer** tab, you can see an option called **Fill Screen** at the top-right corner of the visual designer. Click on that and change it to **Custom**:

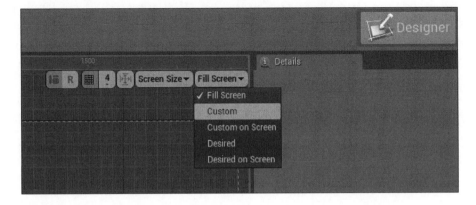

The **Custom** mode will let you assign the width and height of this widget. Let's set the width and height to 256 and 32. Now, we will drag and drop a new Progress Bar into the visual designer and use the following settings:

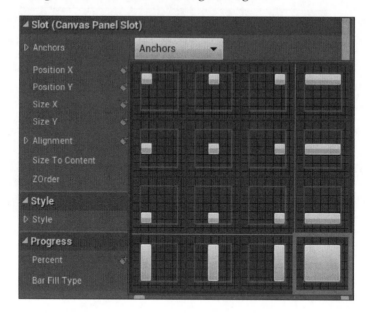

Set the **Anchors** to the very last anchor (this is the Fill Anchor). Anchor helps the widget stay in its position with different screen sizes. This avoids the widget being cropped off the screen. In addition to the fill anchor, there are other preset anchors too, such as fill bottom left side, fill right side, fill bottom area, fill top area, top left, center, right corners, and more. Based on the position of your widget, you can select any Anchor you want and, in the game, the widget will be positioned relative to the Anchor position.

In this example, since we set the anchor to fill, Position X and Y and Size X and Y will be replaced with **Offset Left**, **Top**, **Right**, and **Bottom** respectively. Change the **Offset Right** and **Bottom** to 0.0. The Progress Bar will now be properly stretched to the width and height of the visual designer.

Now, let's create a new variable called **My Character** with the type set to your **ThirdPersonCharacter Blueprint** and bind the **Percent** value to your character's **GetHealthPercentage** function. This is the exact same step we performed for our HUD Widget.

After setting the percent value, let's close this **Widget Blueprint** for now and open **ThirdPersonCharacter Blueprint**. Switch to the **Viewport** tab and click on **Add Component** in the **Components** tab and select **Widget Component**:

Once you select it, this widget component will be added to your Player Character. Select the newly added **Widget Component** and in **Details Panel**, set the **Draw Size** to the same size we used for our **MyFloatingHealthbar**, which was 256 and 32. And then set the **Widget Class** to **MyFloatingHealthbar** class and set **Space** to **Screen**. Finally, move the **Widget** to your desired location. In this example, I've set it above the character's head.

For reference, here is the screenshot:

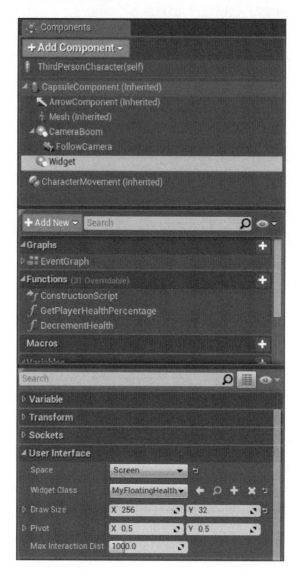

If you play now, you will see the health bar floating on top of the player's head but it will be empty. This is because we haven't assigned the **My Character** value to our floating health bar. To make it work:

1. Switch to the **Construction Script** tab.

2. Right-click anywhere on the **Construction Script** tab, search for **Get Widget**, and select it.

3. Drag a new wire from the **Widget** node you just created, search for **Get User Widget Object**, and select it.

4. Drag a new wire from **Get User Widget Object** Return Value pin, search for **Cast** to **MyFloatingHealthbar**, and select it.

5. Connect the output execution pin of **Construction Script** to this newly created **Cast** node.

6. From the output pin (such as **My Floating Healthbar**) drag a new wire and search for **Set My Character** and select it.

7. Connect the unnamed output execution pin of the **Cast** node to the **Set My Character** node.

8. Right-click on the graph editor, search for `self`, and select **Get a reference to self**. Connect this node to the **My Character** pin.

That's it! Now if you press play, you will see your character's health bar floating on top of your player's head:

Summary

UMG can be used to create a wide variety of UI effects. From here, you can extend this by adding a player portrait image next to your floating health bar or give a weapon to your character and show the ammo count for that weapon and more. You can also add the Widget component to other actors in your game (for example, a treasure chest) that shows information about that actor. Remember that laying out your UI in Visual Designer is only the beginning. To make your UI look good, you have to change the look and feel by changing the style of your widgets.

9
Particles

Particles in Unreal Engine 4 are created using cascade particle editor, which is a powerful and robust editor that allows artists to create visual effects. Cascade editor lets you add and edit various modules that make up the final effect. The primary job of the particle editor is to control the behavior of the particle system itself whereas the look and feel is often controlled by the material.

In this chapter you will learn about the cascade particle editor and create a simple particle system.

Cascade particle editor

To access cascade particle editor, you need to create a **Particle System** in **Content Browser** by right-clicking on the **Content Browser** and selecting **Particle System**. When you select it, a new **Particle System** will be created and it prompts you to rename it. Give it a name and double-click on it to open cascade particle editor.

Once you open it you will see a window like this:

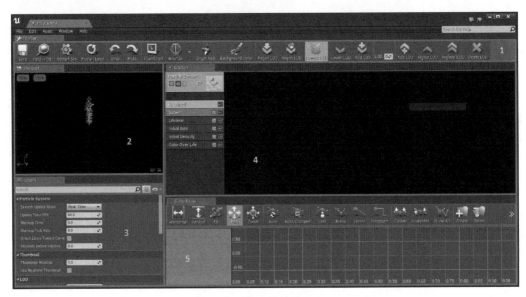

Cascade Editor User Interface

Cascade particle editor consists of five primary areas and they are:

- **Toolbar**: This contains visualization and navigation tools
- **Viewport**: This shows the current particle system
- **Details**: This lets you edit the current particle system, emitter, or modules
- **Emitters**: These are the actual particle emitters and contain modules that are associated with the emitter
- **Curve Editor**: This is the editor that lets you modify properties in either relative or absolute time

Toolbar

Toolbar contains various buttons. Let's take a quick look at them:

- **Save**: This saves the particle system
- **Find in CB**: This locates the current particle system in Content Browser
- **Restart Sim**: This restarts (resets) the current simulation

- **Restart Level**: This is the same as Restart Sim but will also update all the instances placed in level
- **Thumbnail**: This saves the viewport view as a thumbnail for Content Browser
- **Bounds**: This enables or disables rendering of particle bounds
- **Origin Axis**: This displays the origin axis in viewport
- **Regen LOD**: Clicking on this generates the lowest LOD duplicating the highest LOD
- **Regen LOD**: Clicking on this generates the lowest LOD using values based on the highest LOD
- **Lowest LOD**: This switches to the lowest LOD
- **Lower LOD**: This switches to the next lowest LOD
- **Add LOD**: This adds a new LOD before the current LOD
- **Add LOD**: This adds a new LOD after the current LOD
- **Higher LOD**: This selects a higher LOD
- **Highest LOD**: This selects the highest LOD
- **Delete LOD**: This deletes the current LOD

LODs are ways to update the particle effects to use efficient screen space depending on player distance. Based on the effect, there can be modules in a particle system that can be too small to render if the player is far away. Imagine fire embers. If the player is far away, the particle system will still process and calculate these effects which we don't need. This is where we use LODs. **Level of Detail (LODs)** can turn off specific modules or even shut down the emitter based on player distance.

Viewport

Viewport shows you the real-time changes made to the particle system as well as other information's, such as total particle count, bounds, and so on. On the top left corner, you can click on the **View** button to switch between various view modes, such as **Unlit**, **Texture Density**, **Wireframe mode**, and so on.

Navigation

Using the following mouse buttons you can navigate inside the viewport:

- **Left Mouse Button**: This moves the camera around the particle system.
- **Middle Mouse Button**: This pans the camera.
- **Right Mouse Button**: This rotates the camera.
- **Alt + Left Mouse Button**: This orbits the particle system.
- **Alt + Right Mouse Button**: This dollies the camera forward and backward from a particle system.
- **F**: This focus on the particle system.
- **L + Left Mouse**: This rotates the light and only affects particles using **Lit** material. **Unlit** materials have no effect.

Inside the **Viewport**, you can play/pause the particle simulation as well as adjust the simulation speed. You can access these settings under the **Time** option in **Viewport**.

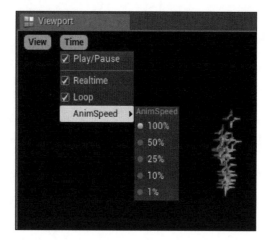

Details

The Details panel is populated by the currently selected module or emitter. The main properties of the particle system can be accessed by selecting nothing in the **Emitters** panel or by right-clicking on the **Emitter** list and navigating to **Particle System | Select Particle System**.

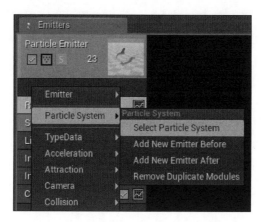

Emitter

The **Emitter** panel is the heart of the particle system, and contains a horizontal arrangement of all the emitters. In each emitter column, you can add different modules to change the look and feel of the particles. You can add as many emitters as you want and each emitter will handle different aspects of the final effect.

An **Emitter** contains three primary areas, and they are as follows:

- On top of the emitter block are the primary properties of the emitter, such as name, type, and so on. You can double-click on the gray area to collapse or expand the emitter column.

- Below that, you can define the type of emitter. If you leave it blank (as in the preceding screenshot), then particles are simulated on the CPU.

- Finally, you can add modules to define how particles look.

Emitter types

Cascade editor has four different emitter types, and they are as follows:

- **Beam Type**: When using this type, the particle will output beams connecting two points. This means you have to define a source point (for example, the emitter itself) and a target point (for example, an actor).

- **GPU Sprite**: Using this type lets you simulate particles on the GPU. Using this emitter lets you simulate and render thousands of particles efficiently.

- **Mesh Type**: When using this, the particle will use actual **Static Mesh** instances for particles. This is pretty useful for simulating destruction effects (for example, debris).

- **Ribbon**: This type indicates that the particle should be like a trail. This means, all particles (in order of their birth) are connected to each other to form ribbons.

Curve editor

This is the standard curve editor that lets the user adjust any values that need to change during the particle's lifetime or across the life of an emitter. To learn more about curve editor, you can visit the official documentation available at `https://docs.unrealengine.com/latest/INT/Engine/UI/CurveEditor/index.html`.

Creating a simple particle system

To create a particle system:

1. Right-click on **Content Browser**.
2. Select **Particle** from the resulting context menu.

3. A new particle system asset will be created in **Content Browser** and prompts you to rename it.

4. For this example, let's call it **MyExampleParticleSystem**.

5. Now, double-click on it to open the **Particle** editor.

By default, Unreal creates a default emitter for you to work with. This emitter contains six modules, and they are:

- **Required**: This contains all the properties required by the emitter, such as the material used to render, how long the emitter should run before looping, can this emitter loop, and so on. You cannot delete this module.

- **Spawn**: This module contains the properties that determine how the particles are spawned. For example, how many particles to spawn per second. You cannot delete this module.

- **Lifetime**: This is the lifetime of the spawned particles.

- **Initial Size**: This sets the initial size of particles when spawning. To modify the size after spawning, use **Size by Life** or **Size by Speed**.

- **Initial Velocity**: This sets the initial velocity (speed) of particles when spawning. To modify the velocity after spawning, use **Velocity/Life**.

- **Color over Life**: This sets the color of a particle over its lifetime.

For this example, we will modify the existing emitter and make it a GPU particle system that looks like sparks. We will also add collisions so that our particles collide with the world.

Creating a simple material

Before we start working with particles, we need to create a simple material that we can apply to the particles. To create a new material:

1. Right-click on **Content Browser** and select **Material**. Feel free to name it anything.

2. Open **Material** editor and change **Blend Mode** to **Translucent**. This is required because GPU particle collision will not work on opaque materials.

3. Then, change **Shading Model** to **Unlit**. This is because we don't want the sparks to be affected by any kind of light since they are emissive.

4. Finally, create a graph like this:

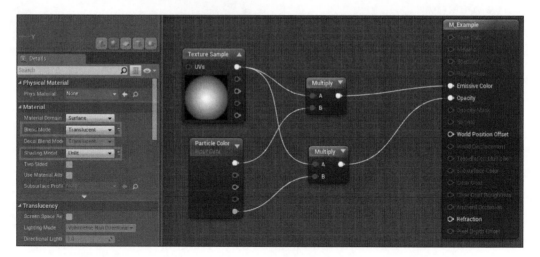

 Note that the circular gradient texture in the **Texture Sample** node comes with the Engine itself. It's called **Greyscale**.

Now that we have our material, it's time to customize our particle system:

1. Select the **Required** module and under the **Emitters** group, apply our material created in the previous step.

2. Right-click on the black area below the emitter and select **New GPU Sprites** under **Type Data**. This will make our emitter simulate particles on GPU.

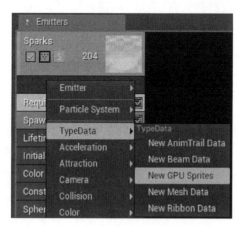

3. Select the **Spawn** module and under the **Spawn** group, set **Rate** to **0**. This is because instead of spawning a certain amount of particles per second, we want to burst hundreds of them in one frame.

4. Under the **Burst** group, add a new entry in **Burst List** and set **Count** to **100** and **Count Low** to **10**. This will select a random value between **100** and **10** and will spawn that many particles.

   The final **Spawn** settings will look like this:

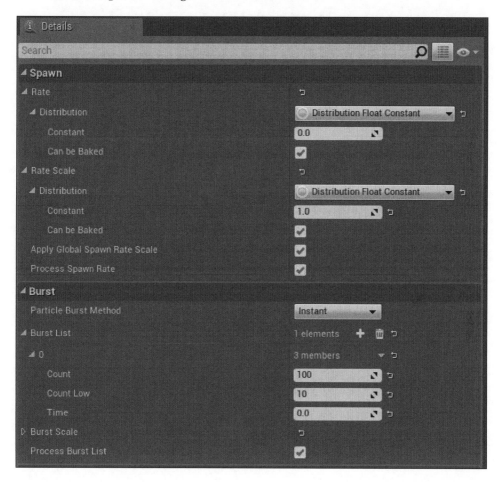

5. After adjusting the **Spawn** settings, we set the **Lifetime** of the particles to **0.4** and **3.0**, so each spawned particles' lifetime is between **0.4** and **3.0**. Now that we have particles spawning, it's time to adjust their size. To do so, select the **Initial Size** module and set **Max** to **1.0, 10.0, 0.0** and **Min** to **0.5, 8.0, 0.0**.

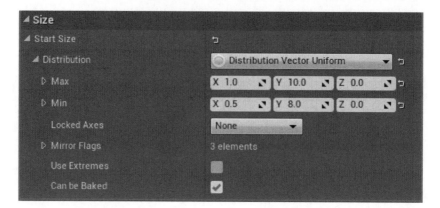

 Note that since GPU sprites are 2D, you can ignore the **Z** value. That's why we set them to **0.0**.

6. After that, select the **Initial Velocity** module and set **Max** to **100.0, 200.0, 200.0** and **Min** to **-100.0, -10.0, 100.0**.

7. Now, if you drag and drop this particle into the world, you will see the particles bursting into the air.

 Note that if you see nothing happening, make sure **Real-Time** is turned on for the editor (*Ctrl+R*).

Adding gravity

In order to make things a bit more real, we will simulate gravity on these particles.
Go back to your particle editor and follow these steps:

1. Right-click on the module area.

2. Select **Const Acceleration** from the **Acceleration** menu. This module will add
    the given acceleration to the existing acceleration of particles and updates the
    current and base velocity.

3. For the **Acceleration** value, use **0.0, 0.0, -450.0**. A negative value of **Z** (that is, **-450**) will make the particles go down as if they are affected by gravity.

 Note that the default gravity value is **-980.0**. You can try this value as well.

Now, if you look at the particle in world, you can see them going down as if they are affected by gravity.

Applying the color over life module

Now that we have something like sparks, let's apply some color to it. Select the Color Over Life module and apply the settings shown here:

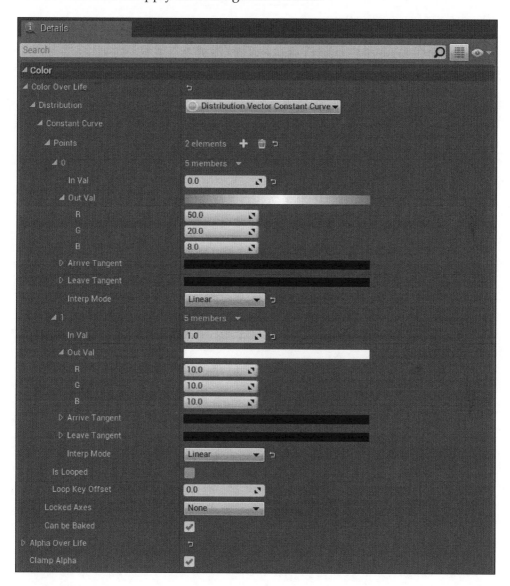

Color Over Life is a curve value. It means you can define what color to apply at a certain point in the lifetime of particle. The **0.0** value is the beginning and **1.0** is the end. In the preceding screenshot, you can see I have applied a bright reddish orange color (**50.0, 20.0, 8.0**) when the particle is spawning (**In Val = 0.0**) and bright white color at the end (**In Val = 1.0**).

Adding collision module

To complete this effect, we will add a **Collision** module so that our particles will collide with the world. To add the **Collision** module, go through the following steps:

1. Right-click on the modules area and select **Collision** from the **Collision** menu.

2. Select the **Collision** module.

3. Set the **Resilience** value to **0.25**. This will make the collided particles less bouncy. Higher resilience means more bouncy particles.

4. Set **Friction** to **0.2**. This will make the particles stick to the ground. A higher friction value (**1.0**) will not let the particle move after colliding, whereas lower values make the particle slide along the surface.

Now, if you simulate or play the game with this particle in the world, you can see it bursting and colliding with the world but it's very unrealistic. You can easily notice that every second this particle keeps repeating. So to prevent this, follow these steps:

1. Open the particle editor.

2. Select the **Required** module.

3. Under the **Duration** settings, set **Emitter Loops** to **1**. By default, this is set to **0**, which means it will loop forever.

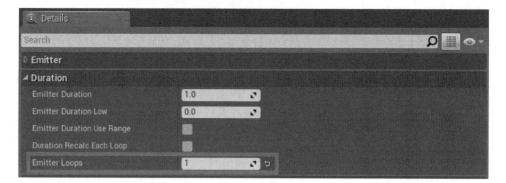

Playing particle in Blueprints

Now that our particle effect is ready, let's play it using Blueprints:

1. Right-click on **Content Browser**.

2. Select the **Blueprint** class.

3. From the resulting window, select **Actor**.

4. Double-click on the **Blueprint** to open the editor.

5. Select your bursting particles in **Content Browser**.

6. Open the **Blueprint** editor and add a new **Particle System Component** (if you select the particle in **Content Browser**, it will automatically set that particle as the template for the **Particle System Component**).

7. Go to the **Event Graph** tab.

8. Right-click anywhere on the graph and select **Add Custom Event...** from the **Add Event** category.

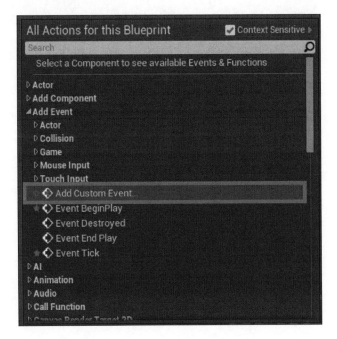

9. Rename that **Custom Event** with any name you like. For this example, I renamed it **ActivateParticle**.

10. Create a graph like this:

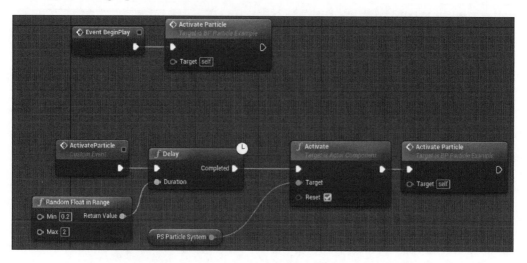

This Blueprint will first execute **ActivateParticle** when the game begins and when the event is executed, it randomly selects a time (in seconds) between **0.2** and **2**. When the time runs out, it activates the particle and calls this event again.

Now, if you drag and drop this particle into the world and start playing, you will see the particles randomly bursting:

Summary

From here, you can extend this particle and add some lights to make it look even more real. Note that the **Light** module cannot be used with GPU particles so you need to create another emitter and add a light module there. Since you learned about the GPU particle data type, you can add more and more emitters that use other data types, such as beam type, mesh type, ribbon type, and so on. From what you learned in this chapter and other chapters, you can create a Blueprint that includes a light mesh that emits this spark particle effect when it receives damage.

In the next chapter, we will dive into the world of C++.

10
Introduction to Unreal C++

In *Chapter 6*, *Blueprints*, you learned about Blueprints, the visual scripting language of Unreal Engine 4. Now you will learn about C++, which can be used to create base classes for Blueprints. In this chapter, you will learn how to create a C++ project (we will use the **Third Person Template**) and modify it to add support for health and health regeneration for our character. You will also learn how to expose variables and functions to Blueprint.

This chapter will be focused on writing C++ code using Visual Studio 2015 in Microsoft Windows.

Setting up Visual Studio 2015

With Unreal Engine 4.10, you will need Visual Studio 2015 to compile C++ for your projects. There are three editions of Visual Studio available. They are:

- **Community edition**: This is free for any individual and nonenterprise organizations for up to five users. For this book, I will be using this edition.

- **Professional edition**: This is a paid version and is useful for small teams.

- **Enterprise edition**: This is for large teams working on projects of any size and complexity.

You can download the Visual Studio 2015 community edition from `https://www.visualstudio.com/downloads/download-visual-studio-vs`

After visiting the above link, select **Community 2015** and choose your format to download. You can either download the web installer or the offline installer. To download the offline installer, select the **ISO** format:

After downloading the setup, double-click on **vs_community.exe** to run the setup and install Visual Studio 2015.

> Before installing Visual Studio 2015, make sure you select **Visual C++** under the **Programming Languages** section. This is required to work with Unreal Engine 4.

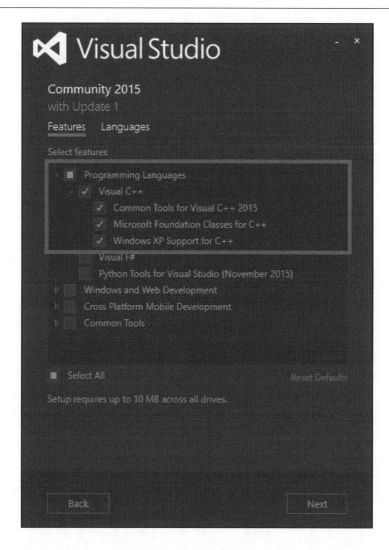

When the installation is complete, the setup will prompt you to restart your computer. Do this, and you are good to go with Unreal Engine 4 C++.

Workflow improvements

There are some recommended settings for Visual Studio 2015 to work with Unreal Engine 4 that improves the overall user experience for developers. Some of them are:

- Turn off **Show Inactive Blocks**. If you do not, many chunks of code may appear grayed out in the text editor. (**Tools | Options | Text Editor | C/C++ | View**).

- Set **Disable External Dependencies Folders** to **True** to hide unneeded folders in the **Solution Explorer**. (**Tools** | **Options** | **Text Editor** | **C/C++** | **Advanced**).

- Turn off **Edit & Continue** features. (**Tools** | **Options** | **Debugging** | **Edit** and click on **Continue**).

- Turn on **IntelliSense**.

Creating a C++ project

Now that we have Visual Studio installed, let's create a project that includes C++ code. In this project, we will extend the Third Person Template that comes with Unreal Engine 4 and add support for health (including health regeneration):

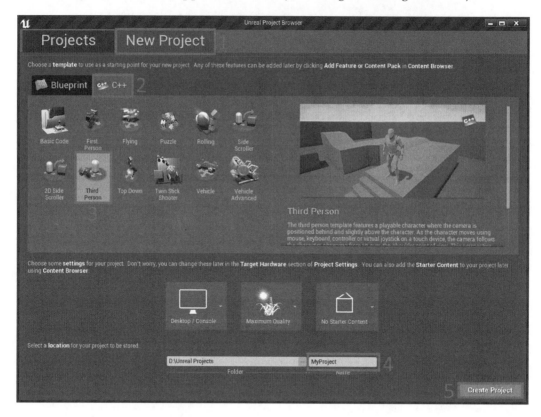

Start Unreal Engine 4 and when the project browser dialog appears:

- Select the **New Project** tab
- Select the **C++** sub tab
- Select **Third Person**
- Name your project
- Click on **Create Project**

When you click on **Create Project**, Unreal Engine 4 will create all the base classes required and will compile the project for you. This might take a minute or so. Once this is completed, the solution file (Visual Studio file) for your project will be automatically opened along with the project.

Once the project is opened, one main change you might notice is the new **Compile** button that appears on the **Toolbar**. This will only appear if your project is a code project:

This is used to recompile the code changes and reload them on the fly, even when you are playing the game! This system is called **Hot Reloading**. As a programmer, you will make use of this feature extensively.

The character class

In this project, we have a character class and a game mode class already available. Let's take a quick look at how the character class is made.

Basically, what we have is a source file (with the extension `.cpp`) and a header file (`.h`). In a nutshell, a header file contains all the declarations, and the source file contains the definitions of those declarations. To access a specific method (or a function) in another file, we use `# include ExampleHeader.h`. This way, we will have access to all functions declared in that header file.

Accessing declarations on another header file are based on access specifiers. We will learn more about them later in this chapter.

To open the source file (.cpp) and header file (.h) from Unreal Engine 4:

- Open **Content Browser**
- Go to **C++ Classes**
- Select your project name folder
- Double-click on your character class

This will open both source file (.cpp) and header file (.h) in Visual Studio:

The preceding screenshot shows the header file of our character class. Let's analyze it line by line.

- `#pragma once`: Any line that is preceded by a hash (#) sign is called a preprocessor directive. Think of it as instruction to the compiler to run before any actual code is compiled. They start with the hash (#) sign and usually ends with a new line. You can have multi-line by using the backslash (\) sign. In this case, `#pragma once` is a preprocessor and its job is to protect against multiple includes. `#pragma once` is known as header guard.

- `#include`: In this file, we see two include files. One is `Character.h` from the `GameFramework` folder (which is in the UE4 directory) and the other is a `generated.h` file:

  ○ `Character.h`: This file is included because our character class is inherited from the `ACharacter` class that comes with Unreal Engine 4. This include is required to access all the declarations in the `Character` class.

  ○ `generated.h`: This is automatically generated for you by **Unreal Header Tool (UHT)**. These are generated whenever you have a USTRUCT() or UCLASS() macro declared. They contain the details of type declarations in your header file. This should be the last include file in your header.

- `Macros`: `Macros` are also preprocessor-directive, which starts with `#define`. Right before the compile time, the compiler copies and pastes the actual values anywhere this macro is used. For example, if you create a macro like this: `#define MyMacro 3.14`, then `3.14` will be copied and pasted everywhere that `MyMacro` is used.

- `UCLASS(config=game)`: This is an Unreal macro that makes the editor aware of the new class. Inside the parentheses, you specify the class specifiers and metadata. In this example, we specify the config specifier. This indicates that this class is allowed to store data in the given configuration file. In this case, the name of your config file will be `YourGameNameGame.ini`.

- `class APACKT_CPPCharacter: public ACharacter`: This indicates the class name and shows you which class we inherited this from. For this class, we inherited it from the `Character` class.

- `GENERATED_BODY()`: This is a macro that must be placed at the very beginning of the class body. When compiling, Unreal will replace it with all the boilerplate code that is necessary. This means that, right before compile time, `GENERATED_BODY()` is replaced by the actual code. Since this chunk of code is required to compile the class, Epic has made it easier for us by creating this macro.

- `private`, `public`, and `protected`: These are called access specifiers. Access specifiers let you decide whether a method can be accessed by other files or not. There are three types of access specifiers. They are:

    ○ `private`: This means you can access the members only in this class. In this example, `CameraBoom` and `FollowCamera` are set as private properties. That means, you can access them `only` inside this class. If you create a new class deriving from this class, you cannot access them.

    ○ `public`: This means all the members can be accessed from any other class.

    ○ `protected`: This means all the members can be accessed from this class and any class that is derived from this class.

- `UPROPERTY()`: This defines the property metadata and specifiers. These are used on properties to serialize, replicate, and expose them to Blueprints. There are a number of `UPROPERTY ()` specifiers that you can use. To see the full list, visit this link: `https://docs.unrealengine.com/latest/INT/Programming/UnrealArchitecture/Reference/Properties/Specifiers/index.html`.

- `void`: This means it's a function that does not return any data type. A function can return any type of data such as `float`, `int`, `bool`, or even objects, but doesn't require a data type all the time. In such cases, you would use the void return type to indicate that this method does not return any type of data. This will also prevent overriding the function in any child classes. If you want to override a function in child classes, then you need to make it a virtual void. When you create a virtual void, it means child classes can override this function, implement their own logic, and optionally call the parent class function using the keyword `Super`.

Understanding the preceding things (preprocessors, macros, access specifiers, and so on) will help a lot as you work in Unreal C++.

Another thing that is worth mentioning is the use of double colons (: :), hyphen arrows (->), and periods (.). Understanding what they are and how to use them is crucial. Out of these, mostly we use the hyphen arrow (->) symbol. Let's see what they are.

- **Double colons** (: :): When using this symbol, it means you are accessing a method from a specific namespace or scope. For example, you will use this symbol when you want to call static methods from other classes.

- **Hyphen arrow** (->): This is used when you are pointing to some data that might or might not exist somewhere in the memory. Using this symbol means you are trying to access a pointer. A pointer points to a location somewhere in the memory where the actual data of that pointer is stored. Before accessing a pointer, it is always a good idea to check them and make sure they are valid. Pointers are one of the most important part in Unreal C++ so I'd highly recommend to read this article provided by Nathan Iyer (Rama): `https://wiki.unrealengine.com/Entry_Level_Guide_to_ UE4_C%2B%2B#Pointers`

- **Period** (.): This is used to access the data itself. For example, you will use this to access the data inside a struct.

Adding the health system

Now that we know about the `Character` class, let's begin by modifying our character to add support for the health and health regeneration system. Before we begin, let's see a quick breakdown of what we will be doing. In this system:

- A `float` variable that holds the current health of the player when the game begins. We will make sure that the player has maximum health when the player is initialized.

- Override the default function `TakeDamage ()` of the `Actor` class.

- When the player is taking damage, we will check how much damage was taken and subtract that amount from the health. We will then start a timer that will execute an event that regenerates health.

Creating a health variable

So let's get started. Open up your character source file and add the following code under private access specifier:

```
UPROPERTY( EditAnywhere, BlueprintReadWrite, Category = "My
Character", meta = (AllowPrivateAccess = "true") )
float Health;
```

Here, we declare a `Health` variable with the data type `float`. We also added `UPROPERTY` to our `float` variable and added the specifiers `EditAnywhere`, `BlueprintReadWrite`, and `Category`. The `EditAnywhere` specifier lets you edit this property in the **Details** panel. `BlueprintReadWrite` allows you to get or set this value in Blueprint. Whatever name you write as the category will appear in the **Details** panel. If you compile and start your game and look at the **Details** panel of the **ThirdPersonCharacter** Blueprint (in **ThirdPersonCPP/Blueprints**) you will see our new property exposed:

As you can see, a value of `0.0` doesn't make sense to `Health`. So what we will do is open the source file of our character class and type the following line under the class constructor:

```
Health = 100.f; // .f is optional. If it's confusing you can replace
it with 100.0
```

The `constructor` class is usually the first definition in a source file. It looks like `YourClassName::YourClassName()`.

 Any line preceded by // (double slash) is a comment and is ignored by the compiler.

The `constructor` class is basically where we set the default values of our class. In this case, we want the default value of our player health to be `100`.

Now, if you press the **Compile** button in Unreal Engine editor, the editor will compile the new changes and hot reload it when it's finished. When the compilation is finished, you should see the new value (which is **100**) as the default value for `health`.

Taking damage

Now that our health is set, we can access it and change it in our `character` class. We now need to update this value whenever our player is taking damage. Since our character is an `Actor` class, we can use the `TakeDamage()` function to update the health. To do so, add the following code to your character header file:

```
virtual float TakeDamage( float Damage, struct FDamageEvent const&
DamageEvent, AController* EventInstigator, AActor* DamageCauser )
override;
```

> *TakeDamage* is a virtual function that already exists in the `Actor` class. So when you want to have custom logic inside virtual functions, make sure you include an override keyword for them. This way you are telling the compiler to look in the parent class for a definition of this function. In case if the base class definition could not be found or has been changed then the compiler will throw an error. Keep in mind that if the override keyword is not there then the compiler will treat this as a new definition.

The `TakeDamage` function takes some parameters and returns a `float` value, which is the actual damage applied. In this function, we will first check whether our health value is larger than 0. If it is, we decrease the `Health` value by the `Damage` value. If not, then we simply return 0:

```
float APACKT_CPPCharacter::TakeDamage(float Damage, struct
FDamageEvent const& DamageEvent, AController* EventInstigator, AActor*
DamageCauser)
{
 // Super key word is used here to call the actual TakeDamage function
from the parent class which returns a float value.We then assign this
value to ActualDamage which is a float type.
 const float ActualDamage = Super::TakeDamage(Damage, DamageEvent,
EventInstigator, DamageCauser);
 // Check if we have health
 if (Health > 0.0)
 {
  // Reduce health by the damage received
  Health = Health - ActualDamage;
  // return the actual damage received
  return ActualDamage;
 }
 // Player has no health. So return 0.0
 return 0.0;
}
```

In the preceding example, you can see the use of comments and how it can help when reading the code later. `TakeDamage` function first calls the parent class function which returns the actual damage to apply. We will save this value to a local variable called `ActualDamage`. We then check whether the `health` value is greater than `0.0` and if it is then `health` value is reduced by the `ActualDamage` float variable and return that value. Whenever you override a virtual function and implement your custom logic, you use `Super::FunctionName()` to inherit the basic functionality of the parent class. Since the `TakeDamage()` function is virtual, and we override that function, we use `Super::TakeDamage()` to call the actual function defined in the parent class, which does the logic of applying damage to the actor.

Health regeneration

Now that our character can take damage, we will modify this system further and add health regeneration. Our health regeneration system will regenerate health based on a `float` variable that is by default set to `1.0` every 1 second, which is also set to a `float` variable. These settings will be exposed to the Blueprint editor, so we can change them later without compiling the game again.

Let's take a quick look at the health regeneration system:

- We use a timer to regenerate health.
- When the player takes damage, we clear this timer.
- After taking damage, we set the timer to restart after 2 seconds. The timer will call a custom function that will regenerate health.
- When the timer finishes, it will call the custom event which will add 1 health. This timer will continue to run until the player reaches maximum health.

So the first thing we need is a `TimerHandle`. This helps in identifying `Timers` that have identical methods bound to them. To declare a `TimerHandle`, open up the character header file and add the following line under `GENERATED_BODY ()`:

```
FTimerHandle TimerHandle_HealthRegen;
```

 You can use any name for `TimerHandle`. Here, the use of `TimerHandle_` before `HealthRegen` is optional.

Since we now know that we will be using timers, let's add two new `float` variables that will act as the time to activate the `RegenerateHealth` function:

- We will call the first `float` variable `InitialDelay`. This is used to call `RegenerateHealth` after taking damage. We will set the default value to 2.
- We will call the second `float` variable `RegenDelay`. When regenerating starts from the `TakeDamage` function, we use this `RegenDelay` time to call the `RegenerateHealth` function again. We will set the default value to 0.5.

The following are the variables:

```
/* After taking damage, Regenerate Health will be called after this
much seconds. */
UPROPERTY( EditAnywhere, Category = "My Character" )
float InitialDelay;

/* Time to regenerate health. */
UPROPERTY( EditAnywhere, Category = "My Character" )
float RegenDelay;
```

We will also add a new property called `RegenerateAmount` and expose it to the Blueprint editor:

```
UPROPERTY( EditAnywhere, BlueprintReadWrite, Category = "My
Character", meta = (AllowPrivateAccess = "true") )
float RegenerateAmount;
```

In the `RegenerateAmount` variable you can see a new meta specifier called `AllowPrivateAccess`. This is used when you want a variable in private access specifier but you need it in Blueprint as well (`BlueprintReadOnly` or `BlueprintReadWrite`). Without `AllowPrivateAccess` compiler will throw an error when you use `BlueprintReadWrite` or `BlueprintReadOnly` on a variable under private access specifier. Finally, we will add a new function called `RegenerateHealth` like this:

```
void RegenerateHealth();
```

For now, we are done with the header file. Let's open the character source file and inside the class constructor (remember the class constructor is `YourClassName::YourClassName()`), add the default value for `RegenerateAmount` as 1.0.

 The constructor class is not construction script in Blueprints. If you want construction script behavior in C++, then you need to override the `OnConstruction` method.

We will also add the `RegenerateHealth` function into our source file like this:

```
void APACKT_CPPCharacter::RegenerateHealth()
{
}
```

Inside this function, we will write our code that will add the `RegenerateAmount` value to our existing health. So let's modify it like this:

```
void APACKT_CPPCharacter::RegenerateHealth()
{
    if (Health >= GetClass()->GetDefaultObject<ABaseCharacter>()-
>Health)
    {
        Health = GetClass()->GetDefaultObject<ABaseCharacter>()-
>Health;
    }
    else
    {
        Health += RegenerateAmount;
        FTimerHandle TimerHandle_ReRunRegenerateHealth;
        GetWorldTimerManager().SetTimer( TimerHandle_
ReRunRegenerateHealth, this, &APACKT_CPPCharacter::RegenerateHealth,
RegenDelay );
    }
}
```

Now, let's analyze that code. The first thing we do inside this function is to check whether our `Health` is greater than or equal to our default `Health`. If it is, we simply set the health value to the default value (which is what we set in the constructor). If it's not, we add `RegenerateAmount` to our existing health and rerun this function using a timer.

Finally, we modify the `TakeDamage` function to add `HealthRegeneration`:

```
float APACKT_CPPCharacter::TakeDamage( float Damage, struct
FDamageEvent const& DamageEvent, AController* EventInstigator, AActor*
DamageCauser )
{
// Get the actual damage applied
 const float ActualDamage = Super::TakeDamage(Damage, DamageEvent,
EventInstigator, DamageCauser);

 if (Health <= 0.0)
 {
  // Player has no health. So return 0.0
```

```
    return 0.0;
}

// Reduce health by the damage received
Health = Health - ActualDamage;

//Is the health reduced to 0 for the first time?
if (Health <= 0.0)
{
 // Clear existing timer
 GetWorldTimerManager().ClearTimer(TimerHandle_HealthRegen);
 return 0.0;
}


// Set a timer to call Regenerate Health function, if it is not
running already
 if (!GetWorldTimerManager().IsTimerActive(TimerHandle_HealthRegen))
 {
  GetWorldTimerManager().SetTimer(TimerHandle_HealthRegen, this,
&APACKT_CPPCharacter::RegenerateHealth, InitialDelay);
 }

// return the actual damage received
 return ActualDamage;
}
```

In the code above, we first check if our health is less than or equal to 0.0. If it is then
we know the player has no health so we simply return 0.0. Otherwise we reduce
our health value and check if health is less than or equal to 0. We clear the timer if
health is 0 otherwise we check if health regeneration is currently active. If it is not
active then we create a new timer to run the RegenerateHealth function and lastly
we return the ActualDamage applied.

C++ to Blueprint

We now have a health and health regeneration system in our character class. One
problem with our current system is that we have not yet defined what happens to
our character after the health reaches 0. In this section, we will create an event that
we will implement in Blueprint. This event will be called when the player's health
reaches 0.0. To create this Blueprint event, open our character header file and
add the following code:

```
UFUNCTION(BlueprintImplementableEvent, Category = "My Character")
void PlayerHealthIsZero();
```

As you can see, we added a normal function called `PlayerHealthIsZero()`. To make this available in Blueprint, we added a `UFUNCTION` specifier and inside that we added `BlueprintImplementableEvent`. This means C++ can call this function and it will execute inside Blueprint but we cannot add a definition for this in our character source file. Instead, we will just call it inside the source file whenever we want. In this example, we will call it inside our `TakeDamage` event if the player's health is `0`. So let's modify our `TakeDamage` like this:

```
float APACKT_CPPCharacter::TakeDamage( float Damage, struct
FDamageEvent const& DamageEvent, AController* EventInstigator, AActor*
DamageCauser )
{
// Get the actual damage applied
 const float ActualDamage = Super::TakeDamage(Damage, DamageEvent,
EventInstigator, DamageCauser);

 if (Health <= 0.0)
 {
  // Player has no health. So return 0.0
  return 0.0;
 }

 // Reduce health by the damage received
 Health = Health - ActualDamage;

 //Is the health reduced to 0 for the first time?
 if (Health <= 0.0)
 {
  // Clear existing timer
  GetWorldTimerManager().ClearTimer(TimerHandle_HealthRegen);

  // Call the BLueprint event
  PlayerHealthIsZero();

  return 0.0;
 }


 // Set a timer to call Regenerate Health function, if it is not
running already
 if (!GetWorldTimerManager().IsTimerActive(TimerHandle_HealthRegen))
 {
```

```
    GetWorldTimerManager().SetTimer(TimerHandle_HealthRegen, this,
&APACKT_CPPCharacter::RegenerateHealth, InitialDelay);
    }


    // return the actual damage received
    return ActualDamage; }
```

In the preceding code, we call PlayerHealthIsZero right after clearing the regen timer.

Now it's time to compile and run the project. In Visual Studio, press *F5* to compile and launch the project. Once the project is loaded, open our character Blueprint and you will see our new variables exposed in the **Details** panel:

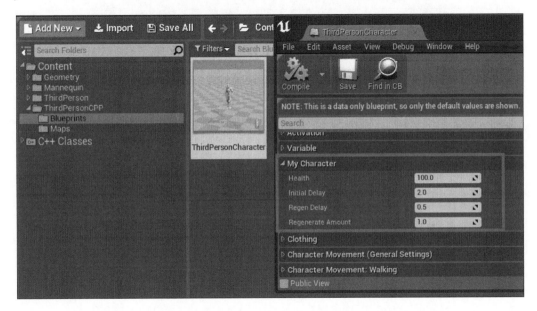

From here, you can open the Blueprint graph and add our **Player Health Is Zero** event:

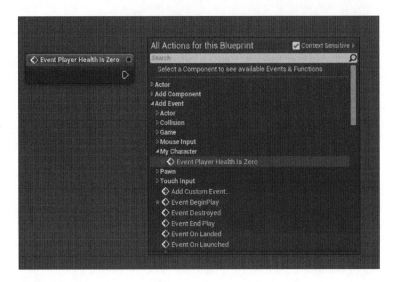

In this event, you can program your logic to play a death animation, show some UI screen, and so on.

Summary

Unreal C++ is easy to learn compared to actual C++. This is because the programming wizards at Epic Games implemented so many features that makes writing Unreal C++ fun! You can extend what you learned from this chapter by including Armor system, Stamina system, and so on for your character. By incorporating UMG and Blueprints, you can show a HUD that shows player health and maybe a small warning system that pops up when the player's health goes below 50. In the next chapter, you will learn how to package a project for shipping.

11
Packaging Project

Throughout this book, you learned the basics of Unreal Engine 4. In this final chapter, we will recap all that, as well as see how to package your project into a standalone game. You will also learn how to package the game for quick distribution and package a game as a release version.

Recap

In the first chapter, you learned the difference between Unreal Engine versions. As I have mentioned, the launcher version is a binary version compiled by Epic and is ready for you to use. But, if you want to get the latest build that is not yet available through launcher, then your only choice is getting the source code from GitHub. If you are going for the source code version of Unreal Engine then I recommend getting the source from the promoted branch. Epic works hard on the promoted build for their artists and designers, so most of the time it is updated daily and you get the latest stuff too! if you really want to get your hands dirty or you have that urge to grab the latest and the most cutting-edge build, then you should go for the master branch. Keep in mind that this branch tracks live changes directly from Epic, it might be buggy and it might even fail to compile.

Once you get the engine up and running, you can start importing your assets into **Content Browser**. This is where you save and edit the assets that are used in your game. **Content Browser** offers a lot of functionality such as searching based on keyword, tags, asset type, filters, etc. and you can use the **Collections** feature in **Content Browser** to add references to your most commonly used assets. When searching, you can exclude specific keywords by adding the hyphen (-) before the name. For example, if you want to exclude all assets that contain the name `floor`, then you can search in **Content Browser** as `-floor`. This will show you all assets that do not contain the word floor.

Another great feature of **Content Browser** is the **Developers** folder. This is especially useful when you are working in a team where you want to try out different techniques or assets in your game without affecting other parts. One thing to remember is that you should only use this strictly for personal or experimental work and you should never include references to external assets outside this folder. For example, if you made an asset that you want to try out before adding it to the game, then you can create a test level inside your **Developers** folder and test out everything there. Think of the **Developers** folder as your own private playground where you can do whatever you want without affecting others work. The **Developers** folder is not enabled by default. To enable it, click on **View Options** at the bottom right corner of your **Content Browser** and select **Show Developers Folder**:

Once you enable that, you will see a new folder called **Developers** under your **Content** folder in **Content Browser**:

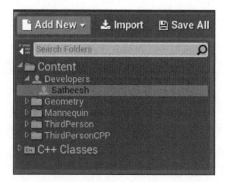

The name of the folder inside the **Developers** folder is automatically set to your Windows username. If you are using **Source Control** (for example, Perforce or Subversion), then you can see the Other **Developers** folder by enabling the **Other Developers** checkbox available under **Filters | Other Filters**:

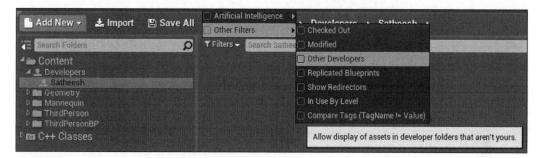

Knowing this will help you a lot when you are working with a team or when you have lots of assets.

Just like how you use **Content Browser** to find assets that are imported, you use **World Outliner** to find assets that are placed in your level. You can also use **Layers** to organize assets that are placed in the level. Both of these windows can be summoned from **Window** in the menu bar:

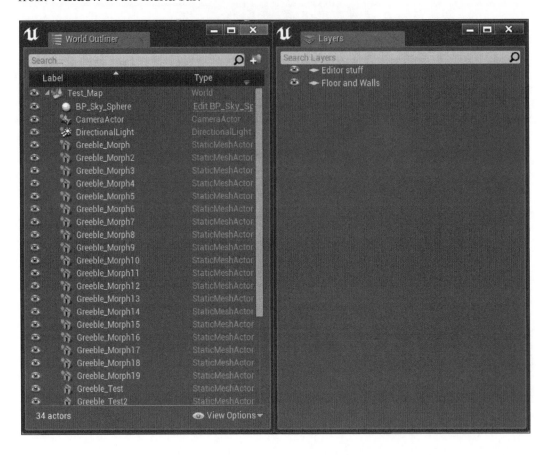

In *Chapter 3, Materials*, you learned about the awesome **Material Editor** and the common nodes that we will use. A good material artist can totally change the realism of your game. Mainly materials and post processing gives you the power to make the game look realistic or cartoony. The common material expressions that we learned are not just used for coloring your assets. For example, create the following material network and apply to a simple mesh (for example, a sphere) and see what happens:

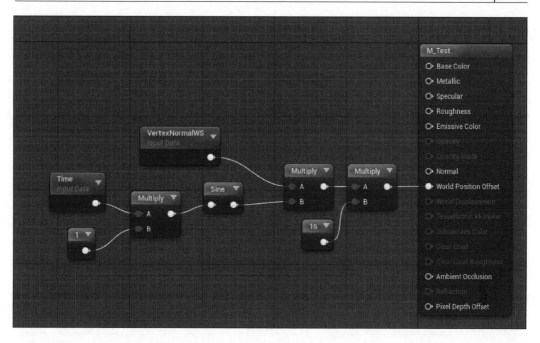

If you find yourself using a specific network multiple times, then it's better for you to create a material function which can tidy up your graph and make it more organized.

As you continue developing your game, you will eventually start tweaking with **Post Process Volume**. This lets you modify the overall look and feel of your game. By combining **Post Process** in blueprints or C++ you can even use it to affect your game play too. A perfect example for this is the detective vision from the Batman Arkham series games. You can use materials in post process to highlight a specific object in world or even use it to render outlines for meshes that are behind other objects.

Another crucial part of the game that determines the final look is lighting. In this book, you learned about different light mobilities, the differences between them including common light settings and how it affects the game world. You also learned about Lightmass Global Illumination which is the static global illumination solver developed by Epic Games.

As you know by now, Lightmass is used to bake lighting and because of that, dynamic lights are not supported by Lightmass. When using Lightmass for your game, you need to make sure that you have a second UV channel for all your static meshes (that are not set to movable) to have proper shadows. If you want to use dynamic lights (that means lights that can change any of their properties at runtime-think of the day and night cycle as an example), Epic has included support for **Light Propagation Volume (LPV)**. At the time of writing this book, LPV is in experimental stage and is not yet ready for production. One extra thing that is worth mentioning here is the ability to change bounced lighting color. Take a look at the following material network:

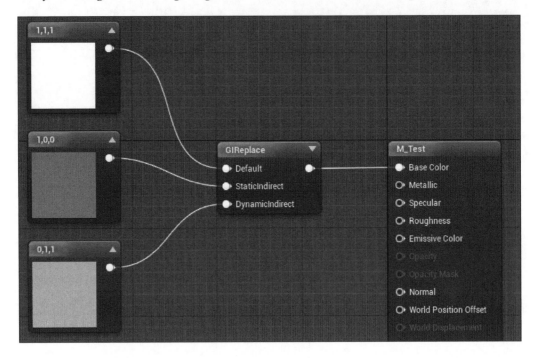

Using the **GIReplace** material node, you can change the color of the bounced light. If you apply the preceding material to a mesh and use Lightmass to build lighting, the result of the bounced light will be red color instead of white. Even though we don't need to have a different color for bounced lights, we can still use this node to darken or brighten the bounced lighting without the need to adjust Lightmass settings.

Once we have all the base setups, we then jump to Blueprints. **Blueprint Visual Scripting** is a powerful and flexible node-based editor that lets artists and designers quickly prototype their game. Mainly, we work with two common Blueprint types and they are **Level Blueprint** and **Class Blueprint**. Inside these Blueprints, we have Event Graph, Function Graph, and Macro Graph. In **Class Blueprints**, we add components to define what that Blueprint is and how they behave. Nodes in Blueprint have various colors applied to them to indicate what kind of node they are. Once you start using Blueprints, you will get familiar with all the node colors and what they mean. We saw how to create a **Class Blueprint** from an `Actor` class and how to spawn it dynamically in the game. We also saw how we can interact with objects in world through **Level Blueprint**. We placed triggers in the level and in **Level Blueprint** we created overlap events for these triggers and learned how to play a Matinee sequence.

Matinee is one of the powerful tools in Unreal Engine 4 that is mainly used to create cinematics. You learned about Matinee UI and how to create a basic cut scene. Since Matinee is similar to other nonlinear video editors, it is easy for video editing professionals to get familiar with Matinee. Even though Matinee is used for cinematics, you can also use it for gameplay-related elements such as opening doors, elevator movement etc.. You can even use it to export your existing cinematics as image sequences or in the AVI format.

After learning about Matinee, we continued to the next chapter to learn about **Unreal Motion Graphics (UMG)**. UMG is a UI authoring tool developed by Epic. Using UMG, we created a simple HUD for the player and learned how to communicate with the player Blueprint to show a health bar for the player. We also made a 3D widget for the player that floats on top of the character's head.

Continuing from there, you learned more about the Cascade Particle System. You learned about Particle Editor and various other windows available inside Cascade Editor. After learning the basics, you created a basic particle system using GPU Sprites including collision. Lastly, we took the particle system to Blueprints and learned how to randomly burst the particles using Custom events and delay node.

Finally, we dived into the magic world of C++. There you learned about various versions of Visual Studio 2015 and how to download Visual Studio 2015 Community Edition. Once we have the IDE installed, we created a new C++ project based on the Third Person template. From there we extended it to include health and health regeneration for our character class. You also learned how to expose variables and functions to Blueprints and how to access them in Blueprints.

Packaging the project

Now that you have learned most of the basics of Unreal Engine 4, let's see how to package your game. Before we package the game, we need to make sure that we set a default map for our game which will be loaded when your packaged game starts. You can set the **Game Default Map** option from the **Project Settings** window. For example, you can set the **Game Default Map** option to your main menu map:

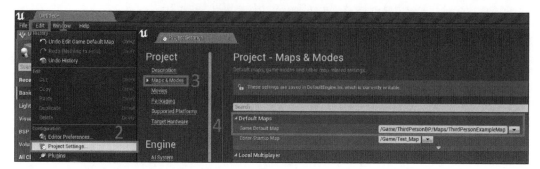

To set a default map for the game, please follow these steps:

1. Click on the **Edit** menu.
2. Click on **Project Settings**.
3. Select **Maps & Modes**.
4. Choose your new map in **Game Default Map**.

Quick packaging

Once you set the **Game Default Map** option, you need to select the **Build Configuration**:

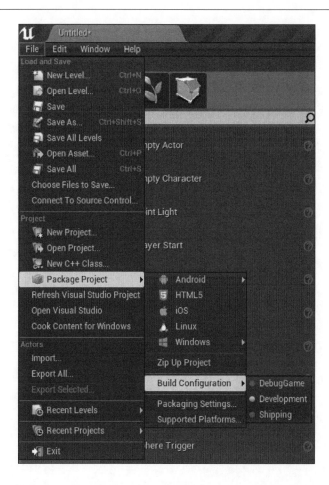

There are three types of build configurations available Packaging the project:

- DebugGame: This configuration will include all the debug information. For testing purposes, you can use this configuration.

- Development: This configuration offers better performance compared to the DebugGame configuration build because of minimal debugging support.

- Shipping: This should be the setting you should choose when you want to distribute the game.

Once you have selected your build configuration, you can package your game from **File | Package Project** and then select your platform. For example, here is the option to package your game for **Windows 64-bit**:

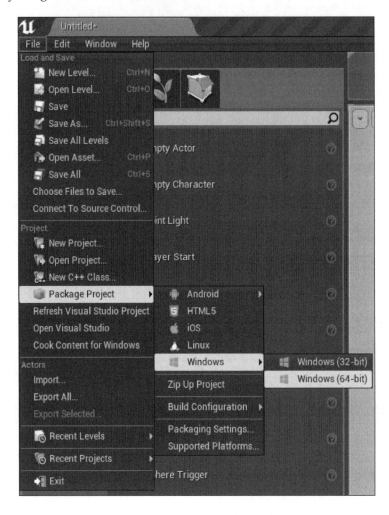

Once you select that option, editor might prompt you to select a target directory to save the packaged game. Once you set the path, editor will start building and cooking the content for the selected platform. If the packaging is successful, you will see the packaged game under the target directory you set earlier.

Packaging the release version

The previously mentioned method is for quickly packaging and distributing the game to end users. However the preceding method cannot build DLCs or patches for your game so in this section, you will learn how to create a release version for your game.

To start let's first open the **Project Launcher** window. **Project Launcher** provides advanced workflows to packaging your game:

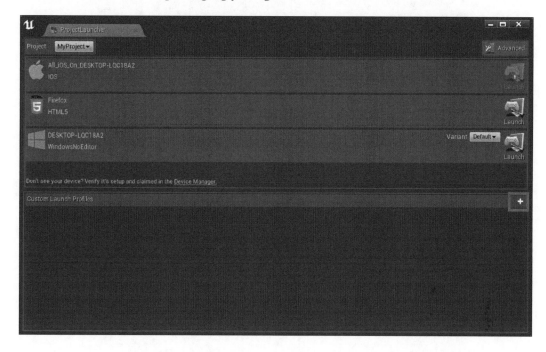

To create a custom launch profile, click on the plus (**+**) button as shown in the preceding screenshot. Once you click on that you will see a new window with new settings as follows:

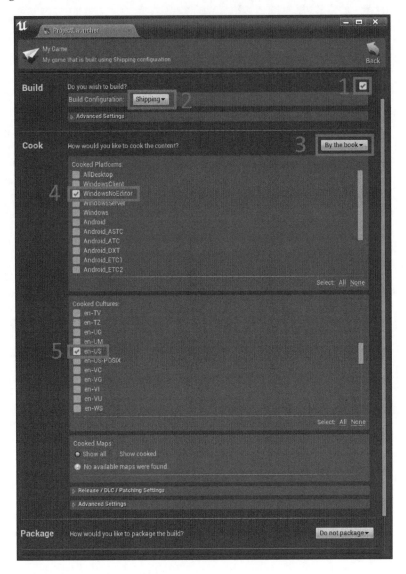

In the preceding window, do the following:

1. Enable the **Build** checkbox.

2. Set the **Build Configuration** option to **Shipping**.

3. Set the dropdown to **By the book**.

4. In this example we selected **WindowsNoEditor** to test on Windows.

5. Select the culture. This is used for localization. By default, **en-US** is selected.

Once all those settings are done, expand the **Release/DLC/Patching Settings** and **Advanced Settings** sections:

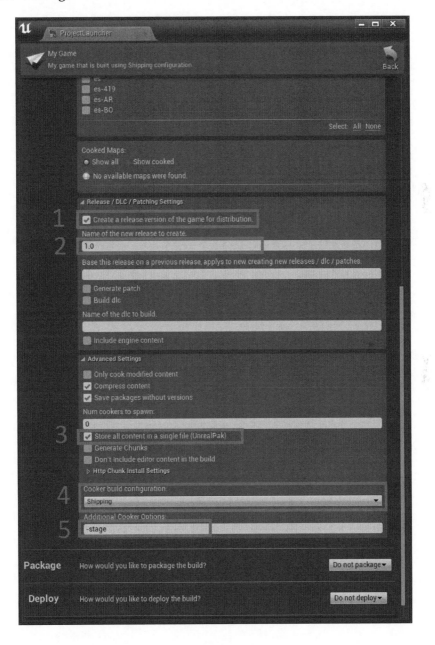

Inside those sections do the following:

1. Enable **Create a release version of the game for distribution**.
2. Set the name of the new release to **1.0**.
3. Enable **Store all content in a single file (UnrealPak)**.
4. Set the **Cooker build configuration** section to **Shipping**.
5. Add the -stage command line as **Additional Cooker Option**. Note that you do not press enter after typing it. Simply click anywhere else to apply that command.

After setting this, set the last two options of **Package** and **Deploy** to **Do not package** and **Do not deploy** respectively:

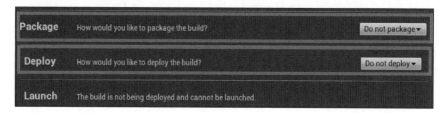

Once all those are done, click on the **Back** button on the top right corner of the **Project Launcher** window and you will see your new profile ready to build:

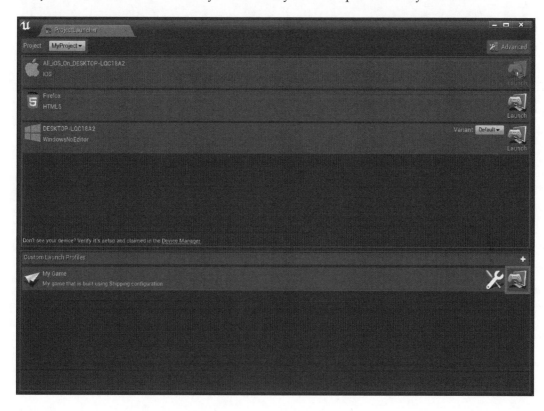

Simply click on the **Launch** button, **ProjectLauncher** will build, cook, and package your game. This might take time depending on the complexity of your game:

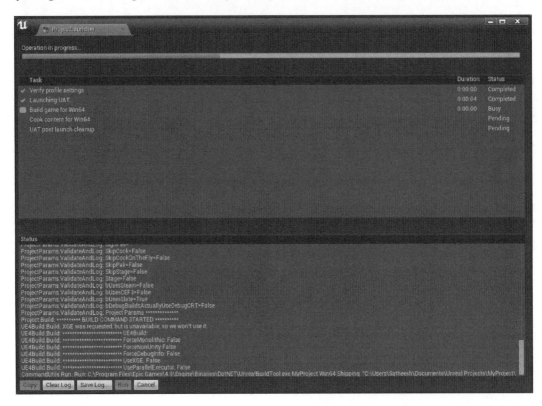

If the packaging was successful, then you can see that in the **ProjectLauncher** window:

You can find your packaged game in your project folder under **Saved |
StagedBuilds | WindowsNoEditor** folder. Now you can distribute this
packaged game to other users.

Summary

Throughout this book, you learned the basics of Unreal Engine 4. We started this
journey with you learning how to download the engine and saw how to import your
own assets. From there you learned about Material Editor and its common aspects.
Then you learned about Post Process, how to use lights and the importance of lights
in video games. You also learned about Blueprints which is the visual scripting
language of Unreal Engine 4. We continued our journey from Blueprints to UMG
which you can use to create any kind of menu in the game. Since a game is nothing
without visual effects and cut scenes, you learned about Cascade Particle Editor
and Matinee. From there we dived into the world of C++ to learn the basics of this
awesome language. Finally you learned how to package the game and distribute
it to others.

References

Your journey of learning Unreal Engine 4 does not stop here. You can extend your knowledge even further by visiting these links:

- *Unreal Engine Community*

  `https://forums.unrealengine.com/`

- *Unreal Engine Official Twitch Streams*

  `http://www.twitch.tv/unrealengine`

- *Unreal Engine YouTube channel*

  `https://www.youtube.com/user/UnrealDevelopmentKit/videos`

- *Unreal Engine AnswerHub*

  `https://answers.unrealengine.com/index.html`

- *Unreal Engine Documentation*

  `https://docs.unrealengine.com/latest/INT/GettingStarted/index.html`

Index

T

TakeDamage function 211
Third Person Template 201
Time Bar 151
toolbar, cascade particle editor
  buttons 184, 185
Toolbar panel
  about 36-38
  Live nodes 40
  Live preview 39
  Live update 40

U

Unreal Box (UB) 23
Unreal Convex (UCX) 24
Unreal Engine 4
  about 1
  AnswerHub, URL 236
  collision generator 24
  community, URL 236
  compiling 5
  Content Browser 11
  custom build, starting 5
  Details panel 14
  documentation, URL 236
  downloading 1
  exploring 5-7
  GitHub version 1
  GitHub version, downloading 3
  launcher (binary) version 1
  launcher (binary) version, downloading 2
  launcher build, starting 5-8
  modes 10
  Official Twitch Streams, URL 236
  URL 2, 3
  viewport toolbar 8, 9
  YouTube channel, URL 236

Unreal Header Tool (UHT) 207
Unreal Motion Graphics (UMG) 167, 225
Unreal Sphere (USP) 24
Unreal Units (UU) 22

V

viewport, cascade particle editor
  about 185
  navigation 186
viewport toolbar
  about 8, 9
  navigating 14
  URL 15
Visual Studio 2015
  setting up 201-203
  URL 201
  workflow improvements 203

W

Widget Blueprint 167

Thank you for buying
Unreal Engine 4 Game Development Essentials

About Packt Publishing

Packt, pronounced 'packed', published its first book, *Mastering phpMyAdmin for Effective MySQL Management*, in April 2004, and subsequently continued to specialize in publishing highly focused books on specific technologies and solutions.

Our books and publications share the experiences of your fellow IT professionals in adapting and customizing today's systems, applications, and frameworks. Our solution-based books give you the knowledge and power to customize the software and technologies you're using to get the job done. Packt books are more specific and less general than the IT books you have seen in the past. Our unique business model allows us to bring you more focused information, giving you more of what you need to know, and less of what you don't.

Packt is a modern yet unique publishing company that focuses on producing quality, cutting-edge books for communities of developers, administrators, and newbies alike. For more information, please visit our website at www.packtpub.com.

Writing for Packt

We welcome all inquiries from people who are interested in authoring. Book proposals should be sent to author@packtpub.com. If your book idea is still at an early stage and you would like to discuss it first before writing a formal book proposal, then please contact us; one of our commissioning editors will get in touch with you.

We're not just looking for published authors; if you have strong technical skills but no writing experience, our experienced editors can help you develop a writing career, or simply get some additional reward for your expertise.

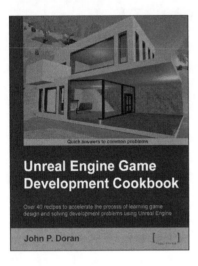

Unreal Engine Game Development Cookbook

ISBN: 978-1-78439-816-3   Paperback: 326 pages

Over 40 recipes to accelerate the process of learning game design and solving development problems using Unreal Engine

1. Explore the quickest way to tackle common challenges faced in Unreal Engine.

2. Create your own content, levels, light scenes, and materials, and work with Blueprints and C++ scripting.

3. An intermediate, fast-paced Unreal Engine guide with targeted recipes to design games within its framework.

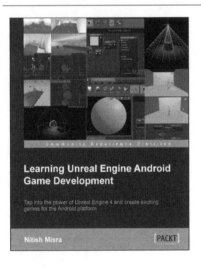

Learning Unreal Engine Android Game Development

ISBN: 978-1-78439-436-3   Paperback: 300 pages

Tap into the power of Unreal Engine 4 and create exciting games for the Android platform

1. Dive straight into making fully functional Android games with this hands-on guide.

2. Learn about the entire Android pipeline, from game creation to game submission.

3. Use Unreal 4 to create a first person puzzle game.

Please check **www.PacktPub.com** for information on our titles

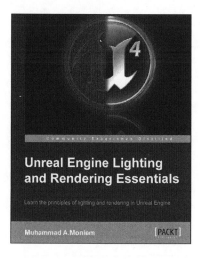

Unreal Engine Lighting and Rendering Essential

ISBN: 978-1-78528-906-4   Paperback: 242 pages

Learn the principles of lighting and rendering in the Unreal Engine

1. Get acquainted with the concepts of lighting and rendering specific to Unreal.

2. Use new features such as Realistic Rendering and Foliage Shading to breathe new life into your projects.

3. A fast-paced guide to help you learn lighting and rendering concepts in Unreal.

Learning Unreal® Engine iOS Game Development

ISBN: 978-1-78439-771-5   Paperback: 212 pages

Create exciting iOS games with the power of the newUnreal® Engine 4 subsystems

1. Learn about the entire iOS pipeline, from game creation to game submission.

2. Develop exciting iOS games with the Unreal Engine 4.x toolset.

3. Step-by-step tutorials to build optimized iOS games.

Please check **www.PacktPub.com** for information on our titles